To Ral[illegible]

Best Wishes!

Bo Diggs

You Gotta Have the Want To

10.95

You Gotta Have the Want To

Allan C. Oggs, Sr.
with
Sherry Andrews

WORD PUBLISHING
Dallas · London · Sydney · Singapore

YOU GOTTA HAVE THE WANT-TO

 The author is indebted to William Manchester's book, *The Glory and the Dream*, for the description of the year 1935 in Chapter 1.

Library of Congress Cataloging in Publication Data

Oggs, Allan C.
You gotta have the want-to.

1. Oggs, Allan C.—Health. 2. Cerebral palsied—United States—Biography. 3. Pentecostal churches—United States—Clergy—Biography. I. Sherry Andrews, 1953- II. Title.
RC388.036 1987 289.9'4'0924 87-2178
ISBN 0-8499-3146-0

89801239 RRD 987654321

Printed in the United States of America

Dedicated to the women in my world:

My lovely wife GWENELDA,
two daughters DEBRA and JODY,
my mother VIOLET,
and daughter-in-law CHERYL.

Contents

Introduction: It's Never Over

IT SEEMED UNBELIEVABLE. The large, graceful chandeliers suspended from the vaulted ceiling of the Hyatt Regency ballroom cast a subdued glow over the room, the crystal and silver dishes glittered pleasantly. A rippling buzz of voices mingled with Muzak as white-jacketed waiters moved unobtrusively among the dinner guests. You would think all that elegance would say loud and clear, "Relax, you are not still climbing the mountain . . . you are straddling its peak." But, no, I was still strung as tight as a piano wire.

Sitting at the head table, I was acutely aware that I was the object of restrained, but intense scrutiny. Although no one was impolite enough to stare, I caught the furtive glances, the discreet gestures, and it made me more self-conscious than usual. Although I tried to cover my nervousness, I could feel the sweat trickling down between my shoulder blades. I was horrified when the wife of my host said, "Allan, you're so warm, take off your jacket." O *no*, I thought, *she sees me sweating.*

The seating arrangement increased my anxiety. With my spastic right arm, being boxed in between two people was sheer misery. I really needed to sit at the end of the table where I could get my arm out of the way. But as the guest of honor, I was front and center. That left me with two choices: I could either pick around in my food, pretending to eat, or try to make light of the situation by warning my dinner companions to defend themselves.

If I chose the latter, I would be faced with a formidable array of china, crystal and silverware, lying in ambush, which I would have to master. If the water glass was not placed perfectly I courted disaster with every sip. At one dinner I had dropped and broken three glasses. Fortunately, they were not expensive, but the host had been upset nonetheless. He had told the other guests, "If he comes to your place, give him a tin cup." Although I had never done that before or since, the memory of it haunted me every time I attended a formal dinner. Often I have suffered through an entire meal thirsty, but afraid to try to drink because the glass was in the wrong place.

Tonight, I was too busy concentrating on other potential hazards to worry much about eating. While making small talk with the guests around me, I was secretly plotting the best path from my seat to the podium, watching to see if it was stable, as the host made introductions and announcements.

While dozens of people crowded around, exclaiming how blessed they had been by hearing me on Dr. James Dobson's "Focus on the Family" radio show, I was worrying about how to appear normal when I made my move on the platform.

Of course, when I got there, I wasn't normal. Since the podium was not anchored, I stood stiffly, placing my right arm behind my back and grasping it tightly with my left to hold it down. Looking out at the sea of curious, expectant faces, I prayed that I would be able to communicate with them as I have been communicating with church congregations and audiences for more than thirty-three years. I began tightly, and a little hesitantly. But, it happened again! Before I had gotten very far into my talk, I felt the anointing of the Holy Spirit wash over me again . . . "the Word was becoming flesh again." I knew then that everything would be fine.

Preaching had been the grand obsession of my life since that night more than thirty years ago, when I had stepped into the pulpit for the first time, and felt the rush of that anointing, transforming me from a spastic teenager with a speech impediment, into a preacher with power. From then on, I had lived to preach, to experience that anointing, which never failed to fill me with an awesome sense of the power of God. When I am under the anointing, anything seems possible. Fatigue, shyness, physical defects, disappear from my consciousness. I could feel like a tiger in the pulpit. Years later, when I pastored, I would try to schedule and handle serious crises soon after church services, while the anointing was still resting strong upon me.

Outside of the pulpit, and the anointing, everything I did had to be seasoned with a "grand coping strategy." Nothing came easily. It never had. All my life I had struggled against the debilitating, crippling effects of cerebral palsy. I have never "adjusted" to my handicap. Instead I have worked hard to overcome it.

By nature and training, I am a relentless optimist. If you commit your life to God, I believe, there is nothing you cannot accomplish if you have a strong enough "want-to" and are willing to work. I am living proof that it works. I have achieved far more than anyone could have expected or dreamed possible. But occasionally I wonder if maybe I haven't been a little too successful. I have coped so well with my handicap that few people suspect how much it can still hurt.

At a General Conference in Fort Worth, Texas, I spoke a few words across the aisle to a young preacher whom I had known for most of his life. I could tell that in the noise and confusion of the convention, my words were lost. I ached when I overheard the young preacher say to his friend, "I don't know what he said. It sounded like a foreign language to me."

My lack of coordination shows up most clearly when I am eating. While I was having lunch at a shopping center cafeteria, a weird, unkempt woman, whom I had noticed many times because of her repulsive eating habits, approached my table. In a very loud, dramatic voice she said, "Every time I see someone like you, I thank my God for making me normal." She drew the attention of the entire section to my table. I tried to move her on, but she continued her loud thanksgiving. Finally, in exasperation, I asked her, "Lady, I don't know who you are, but really, are you suggesting to me that you are normal?"

Normal. I have tripped over that word all my life. I have often mused about what it meant to be normal. Why was it that someone who walked with an unsteady gait was declared abnormal, while an obnoxious or immoral person with a perfect body was considered normal?

When I had displayed my usual nervousness before speaking to a regional meeting of the Full Gospel Businessmen's Fellowship International, my wife gently reminded me, "Remember, honey, if you weren't crippled, they wouldn't have asked you to speak." I knew she was right, but I was still haunted by that word, "crippled." I had two ambitions in life, to be a great preacher and to be normal.

On my best days, I felt that I had achieved the former (humility would not let me claim greatness, but I knew in my heart that I was a good preacher). I could still aim for the latter. Sometimes, I can even joke about my handicap.

While serving on a committee to plan a Youth Day for my denomination, the president of the Youth Division, Donald Deck, had said, "Let's have a healing service." Then looking at me with eyes full of mischief, he added, "Oggs, I want to see you in that prayer line. We want to get you straightened out." I answered, "Not on your life. You're not going to ruin my ministry." Deck would always declare that on the day he hired me he had just seen a giant sign that said, "Hire the handicapped."

Another time, late at night, when returning home from a long day, I had evidently weaved my little VW across the center line, and was stopped by a state trooper. After seeing the weave and hearing me talk, the trooper said, "You're drunk!" I answered, "You're out of your mind. I'm a preacher." The trooper asked if I'd like to guess how many times he had gotten that answer. We argued. "Get out of the car and let me see you walk a straight line." I said, "I'll do it, but be sure I get your name and your badge number because I'm gonna get your job, your car, your house, and maybe your wife, for what you are subjecting me to." I smiled and walked the line in my spastic way, convincing the trooper more than ever, "You are drunk."

But even when I could laugh at myself, my laughter was tempered by the knowledge that for a handicapped person, the battle is never over.

In Ocean Springs, Mississippi, the pastor asked me if I would encourage the parents of a little girl who had been hideously scarred in a house fire. "I think they would listen to you, because you have overcome your handicap." The pastor was stunned when I answered, "Who says I have overcome? I am still in the process of overcoming it."

God and my "want-to" have brought me a long way. Where I will go from here, no one knows.

Grandma and Grandpa Oggs

The twins, Nellie Daisy
and Jessie Buttercup

Grandma VanHorssen—Grandmas are supposed to be big and soft

About three years old

You Gotta Have the Want To

1

Good Ground

I BEGAN TO STAKE OUT my place in 1935, a year America was waking and stretching from the long Depression nightmare. Benny Goodman, a forty-dollar-a-week clarinetist, wasn't having much luck. He decided to use the swing rhythm and thus the twenty-five-year-old Goodman became, overnight, the king of swing. Frank Sinatra was still plugging away at $25 a week singing, "All or Nothing at All." The Lindbergh kidnaper was captured with $13,759 of the ransom found in his Bronx home. The Lone Ranger was being heard three times a week by twenty million people on one hundred and forty radio stations. And Shirley Temple was only ten years old.

Samson and his riddle, "out of the eater came forth meat," described perfectly the condition of the post-depression era. The Great Depression wrinkled and broke a lot of good men. More than 5,000 American banks fell and the wages of those who had jobs averaged $16.21 per week. In September, 1932, there were an estimated 34 million men, women and children who were without any income whatever—nearly 28 percent of the population. In Philadelphia, so many families were put on the street that little girls invented a doll game called "eviction."

"These unhappy times," said Franklin D. Roosevelt, "call for the building of plans that put their faith once more in the forgotten men at the bottom of the economic pyramid." FDR said, "Above all, try something."

There were no power mowers, home air conditioners, automatic dishwashers, clothes dryers, electric blankets, frozen food, automatic coffee makers, xerox machines, scotch tape, home freezers, snow blowers, electric can openers, or refrigerators, only ice boxes.

But from the yet warm belly of an "Eater Depression" came forth a meaty substance that wrapped the bare bones of a nation with the stuff of which good people, good families, dreams and great nations are made.

The beautiful, historic, and quaint city of New Orleans, with its music, parades, Creole food and slow pace will always be my home. New Orleans is divided into four sections—never north, south, east or west—it is always uptown, downtown, lakeside and riverside. Their "English" will only be heard in the city that fills the big crest of the mighty river, the Mississippi.

The uptown area of the city is a mixture of wharfs, factories, universities, mansions and shotgun houses. The shotgun house is unique in New Orleans, where rooms of a house, regardless of the number, are set one behind the other, with all the interior doors in a straight line, so that you could stand on the front porch and shoot a shotgun blast through all the rooms and out the back door. I knew most about the shotgun houses, the parks, and Tchoupitoulas Street.

These gray, stormy, swirling eddies of circumstances and financial crises slammed the Oggs family (four boys, one girl, parents and a great aunt) into the city from Kansas City, Kansas. Each one different, but the same. They each had their individual personalities and preferences concerning the fluffy things of life, but if you squeezed them, put them under pressure, or could sneak into their minds for a peek you would quickly discover that they all had a bedrock of ability. The set of their jaw flashed a warning, "This face bites." Every one of them, in time, would clamp down on their part of life, and with pit-bulldog tenacity, reduce it to digestible proportions.

The man of the house, Theodore A. Oggs, Sr., 6′2″ tall, never weighed more than 165 pounds in his life. A carpenter by trade, a project or building site superintendent, he wore long sleeves at all times to hide his long bony arms. He educated himself, he said, with a Bible in one hand and a newspaper in the other.

Theodore's wife, and mother of the clan, was Nellie Daisy—about 4′11, and somewhat stocky. She was aggressive, feisty, argumentative, a conniver and strategist. But she was also very generous with her love and her means. She had an identical twin, Jessie Buttercup. They often fought, throwing scissors and irons at each other, but they stuck together against outsiders and few dared to take on both of them at the same time.

The boys were Rex, Edward, Theodore Jr. (known as Ted) and Lawrence, who died at an early age. There was a daughter, Viola, who was married so often most lost track of the count.

My dad, Ted, was a very handsome, talented man. A good painter, musician, singer and master carpenter, he became a preacher and pastor of a church at the age of 43. His dealings with his son were always two-handed. The one was kind, a hand of extreme love and caring. The other was careful but tough. When the doctors suggested that his son should wear braces as a child, he answered emphatically, "No." He underscored his decision with hours of personal attention each day of my life. For example, we played endless games of baseball as a means of therapy and when I would not take my gloved left hand and cross it over my body to catch the ball thrown to my right side, my father convinced me to do so by throwing continuously on the right side until he broke the little finger on my right hand.

Only one in my dad's family finished high school. My

dad, Ted, went through eighth grade. He lost an eye shooting papers on a rubber band and that ended his schooling. So all the Oggs were self-made people. Each of them, all four boys and the girl, was talented in his own right. On their own they polished off quite a bit of life for themselves. They were fighters, amongst themselves or otherwise, but they were also a close-knit clan with deep loyalty to each other.

My mother's family consisted of Allan and Clara Van Horssen, my mother Violet, and her sister Myrtle. It was easy to tell by their cooking and dialect that they were natives of New Orleans. Clara claimed to have an ancestry that could be traced back to Queen Victoria of England. My people on Mom's side, to the best of our knowledge, were involved with shipping and the sea. My mother and her older sister, Myrtle, struggled through the chaotic life of a broken home, caused, among other reasons, by their dad being an absolute alcoholic and a drunk. Many days Violet would be accosted by her dad on the way to school and he would take her lunch money to feed the addiction that possessed him. Wonder of wonders, why did she name me after this man who was buried with the unclaimed dead in "Potter's Field," New York City? A man no one was supposed to love. This I've never understood. All the hostility that Violet expressed toward her dad, yet she asked me to share his name.

Clara VanHorssen, unable to cope with her husband's drinking, surrendered to a bad situation. When her marriage failed, she took a lover who supported her and the girls. The girls knew. They had to spend every Sunday afternoon, rain or shine, out of the house, in the park. They kept it a secret until about five years ago. They were both in their sixties by then and they would blame her in one breath and condone her in another—trying their best to love her in spite, or maybe because of, the difficult circumstances of the home.

Clara's surrender created a fierce determination in her girls to survive. Myrtle was just plain tough, although never to her family. She would take on anyone. She supported Violet in whatever way she could, repeating some of her mother's mistakes, because she was determined that her baby sister would not have to struggle. She insisted that Violet stay in school and she got within a few weeks of graduating from high school, when she married Ted Oggs.

Ted and Violet courted in a car with front windows made of cardboard, and married in 1928. Ted was 23, Violet, 16. In December of 1929, all of Ted united with the grit and brute determination, born of the hurt and embarrassment of Violet's twisted and dangerous childhood, to produce a son—Theodore III. The miracle of life pushed its way into the security and warmth of a young woman's body, who had determined in her heart to design and produce something beautiful for her children. They would have the kind of happiness she never knew.

Their home situations created in Ted and Violet a real toughness in determining what they would and would not have in their future. Ted had been raised with a tough bunch of boys who believed that any challenge could be conquered if you worked hard enough, and Violet was resolved that the hurt she had experienced would not be repeated under any circumstances. The fierceness of their combined resolve would be the soil in which my "want-to" would be sown and take root.

The two clans, the Oggs and the VanHorssens, had never been very religious. The Oggs were Episcopalians who never went to church and the VanHorssens had been Catholics for generations, but for them the mass never cleaned up the mess. However, as both families gathered around the calendar to wait for the birth of Violet's second child, the post-Depression baby, they were about to experience a wonderful encounter with God.

The Gospel Tent was stretched on Magazine Street, between Octavia and Joseph Streets. John Baptist (J. B.) Thomas was the preacher. He slept at night on park benches because he couldn't afford better. He wore shoes stuffed with newspapers for inner soles and took his meals wherever he could. The tent, which looked more like a sideshow circus tent than a church, attracted attention in that predominantly Catholic neighborhood. Ted and Violet were among the crowd of curious who gathered "just to look" at what was happening.

But Brother Thomas was a powerful preacher and it wasn't long before Ted and his good friend, Vernon Jaco, were sitting on the platform playing music. By New Year's night, 1935, Ted, who had been half drunk when Teddy III had been christened in the Catholic church, had received the Holy Ghost in this sawdust-floored, canvas-topped cathedral. Violet had not yet received the Holy Spirit, but by New Year's Eve she had been attending services regularly and was pregnant.

One night, while she was sitting on a tent bench, the priest from St. Francis of Assisi Church arrived and began marching up and down the aisles looking for his parishioners. When he saw her, he walked between the benches, took her by the ear, literally, and led her back up the aisle to the street. Then with a kind of flip of his hand he aimed her toward home screaming after her, "Violet, stay away from here. Don't ever come back." And she didn't—until the next night.

The day after she received the Holy Ghost, my mother took her Bible to the priest, full of her new experience and eager to sort things out for her future. She asked, "Is Acts 2:38 in your Bible?" The priest said, "Now daughter, you need to understand . . ." "All I want to know is, is Acts 2:38 in your Bible?" she said. "Well, yes . . . but it's really not for you." She said, "I have a pretty good idea who it's for; I just want to know is it in your book?" "Well, yes, it's in my book." And with great excitement she said, "Not only is it in your book, it is in my heart. Last night I received the wonderful gift of the Holy Spirit!" It couldn't have come at a better time for her, or for the child she was carrying who, for the next fifteen years or so, would require so much of her and Ted's time. The strength of their resolve, their faith, their confidence to lead and guide, would push back barriers and give me the confidence to conquer my limitations.

On September 17, 1935, 10:00 A.M., Allan Charles Oggs was born at 4913 Perrier Street in a four-room-and-a-bath shotgun house. Violet almost died. I was stillborn and suffered severe brain damage. I was rushed to Touro Infirmary. Violet did not believe I was alive. John Thomas prayed for Violet, then went from the Perrier Street house to the hospital, about eight blocks away, to pray for me. I was holding tightly to a thread of life . . . .

John Baptist Thomas
—my very own forerunner

The first grader

5219 Tchoupitoulas St. I spent my first eleven years here

2

Ignorance Is Bliss

THE DOCTOR'S ORIGINAL PROGNOSIS was grim—the baby would probably not survive the first twenty-four hours. If he did, due to extensive brain damage, he would never walk, talk, or see. "My best advice for you is to pray for a merciful death," the attending physician told the distraught Ted. But the doctor hadn't reckoned with J. B. Thomas. It seemed somehow appropriate that a man named John Baptist would make such a forceful appearance at that Jewish hospital. The fiery pentecostal preacher called fervently on the name of the Lord in behalf of his newest brother. He attracted quite a bit of attention! But from that first visit, a detectable change began to take place in my body. It was the beginning of my miracle.

After that first night, Pastor Thomas visited both the hospital and the home twice a day to pray for us. At the same time, a member of the church organized a twenty-four-hour-a-day prayer chain which continued for several days. By the end of the first week it became obvious that I was not going to die, and the doctors had also discovered, to their amazement, that

I was not going to be blind. However, they were still pessimistic about my chances for living any kind of normal life.

Touro Infirmary was a sixteen-block round trip from Perrier Street. Twice a day my grandfather walked from our house to the clinic with milk from my mother for me. She still did not believe I was alive. She was convinced that the rest of the family was engaged in a conspiracy to keep her from discovering the truth. So, one day before she had fully recovered, she sneaked out of the house and walked to Touro to find out the truth. On her way home, she began to hemorrhage. Fortunately, the family, alarmed at discovering her gone, had suspected the truth and struck out immediately toward the infirmary to find her. Otherwise, she might have died after affirming that her child was, indeed, alive.

After monitoring my condition for several weeks, the doctors decided they could do no more for me, so they allowed Ted and Violet to take me home. There was little knowledge, and less treatment, available for Cerebral Palsy then, so the best advice our family physician, Dr. Herbert, could give my parents was, "Take him home and do the best you can for him."

I'm certain they must have been terrified as they left the hospital with their helpless new son cradled in Violet's arms. They had no C.P.* clinic to turn to for help and there wasn't even much literature available on C.P. Today, they probably would be involved in a support group with other parents of C.P. children. But, except for their families, Ted and Violet were alone. They had only their faith, their courage and their ingenuity to see them through. I'm sure there must have been times, especially in those early years, when they wondered if that were enough. Lying in bed at the end of a particularly frustrating day of coping with my limitations, they must have stared into the darkness and questioned why God let this happen to them. But I never heard them express their doubts or

*Cerebral Palsy

fears openly. Holding tightly to each other, they searched their night for a hint of light.

Other youngsters learned to walk while I learned to crawl, and while they were running, I still stumbled. I'd lurch forward, fling my arms out to try to stabilize my balance and, after a whole lot of pitching back and forth, finally get to my feet. Once up, I would wobble unsteadily for a few feet until I fell again. I fell often and bled plenty, but most of the time I was not picked up. Doctor's orders!

My parents were determined to give me as normal a life as possible and that meant letting me take my share of spills. They spent countless hours working with me, devising exercises to strengthen my legs, discovering through trial and error what forms of therapy were most effective. My father painted a white line down the center of the bedroom which I shared with my brother. It took me months of painstaking practice to be able to walk with anything approaching a straight path along it.

My favorite form of therapy was playing ball with my dad. Every day we spent some time, playing pitch and catch, throwing a softball back and forth in our front yard. One of my throws went so wide of its mark, I busted the windshield of our own car parked at the curb. He would gradually heat up his throw and that would encourage me to throw it harder. He knew how to catch the ball so that it made a popping sound—like it had been thrown hard and made a real impact on the glove. That increased my confidence. I thought, *Man, I'm popping his mitt.* He always seemed to know my limit and we would quit before I got so tired I couldn't throw anymore.

Every few months, my mother and I would walk to Magazine Street, ride the street car to Foucher Street, then get off and walk the next four blocks to the Touro Infirmary. We entered at the charity entrance on Foucher Street. Just inside the door was a big box where they collected silver and aluminum for the war effort. War-time factories recycled our discarded cans and gum wrappers into machine and weapons parts. The doctors at Touro monitored my progress and made suggestions about therapy, but they were unable to add much to my parents' efforts. When they suggested that I wear leg braces, my father responded with an emphatic, "No!"

It wasn't easy for me, and I'm sure it wasn't easy on my parents, but they never complained. And they taught me not to either. I am so glad I didn't know it hurt. I did a lot of laughing because I didn't know I was supposed to cry.

One afternoon at a Sunday school picnic, I fell in the wading pool and cracked open the back of my head. Sister Thomas, the pastor's wife, dressed in (of all things) a white skirt, carried me for a mile or so to the first aid station. By that time the white skirt had turned to crimson red and everyone wondered if maybe I would bleed to death. But after they cleaned me up and stitched my head back together, I was fine—more angry that I had to miss the rest of the picnic than hurt.

Though I was surrounded by strong people who never fell, who never bled or spilled their drinks, or painted the front of their shirts with the color of the daily menu, I was unaware that I was different. My parents were always extending my horizons. There was never any suggestion that I couldn't do some things because I was "crippled." In fact, that word was never used, and to this day you can raise my mother out of her chair by calling her son a cripple. My parents never let me feel sorry for myself, to sit in a corner and pout that *everything's against me, nobody loves me, I'll just go eat worms.* I didn't realize I was doing things that everybody else knew I shouldn't be able to do. I just figured I could, and nobody told me I couldn't.

Of course, my coordination was so poor that mastering even ordinary childhood activities took longer and required more effort. My parents bought me an erector set. It had a bunch of nuts and bolts, which you could use to build bridges—or windmills. I would sit on the floor for hours, trying to build a bridge, trying to put a nut and a screw together. Just as it would seem I had almost accomplished it, without warning my hand would jerk or shake and the nut would fly half-way across the room.

There were hundreds of nuts and screws and I could easily have picked up two more and started over. But instead I would get down on my hands and knees and crawl around the pile of nuts and screws, all the while talking to the nut that was trying to escape: "You aren't going to get away from me. I'm going to get you and I'm going to tighten you down until your ears hurt." It was like one nut talking to another.

I'm sure that anyone watching me would have laughed, but if they had looked beyond my clumsy mannerisms, they would have seen in my fierce determination not to be defeated by a nut, the beginnings of that desire which would eventually help me to overcome bigger obstacles.

It was the same way when I got a bicycle. My mama told me I couldn't have one, but my daddy bought it for me. It was a brand new, shiny red bike and I thought it was the most beautiful thing I had ever seen. My walking was still unstable, but now I was determined to learn to ride. After my first few tries, I looked like a massive glob of bruised scar tissue. I was scraped and bruised and black, blue, and green. I fell everywhere. At the end of the first day I leaned the bike up against the step and said, "You had your day, tomorrow is mine. I'll break you tomorrow. I'll ride you. If I die, right before I die, I'm going to ride you."

The next day was just like the day before. Everybody was holding their breath hoping I wouldn't kill myself. Then I disappeared and after a little while I came round the block and I had the thing upright. I was as stiff as a board, I wouldn't look in either direction, but I was on top and I passed the house and kept on going. When I came back around the second time, I was holding on with one hand and waving with the other.

When I finally just flat ran out of gas, I parked the bike at the step, turned around and laughed like an idiot. I pointed my finger at it and said, "I told you I would." As I walked away, I stopped suddenly, jerked around and said, "What did you say . . . if you don't think I can do it again, I'll get right back on you and do it again."

For the first five years of my life, my parents fought neighbors, sought medical help wherever they could find it, and erected buffer zones for me. But they couldn't shield me from life indefinitely. The first big test of their efforts came when I was enrolled in kindergarten.

Kindergarten was a frightening experience. After several tearful trips I agreed to stay and my first full day I met a lady who was to play a major part in molding my entire life. She herself had never married. She stood ramrod straight and tall. I don't remember her ever touching me, or smiling one time. But she gave something of herself to me—values that could not be measured. Her name was Alma V. Wills. For the next nine years she was my absolute defender.

After a bad beginning, I sailed through kindergarten, even managing to win a "beauty contest" before I graduated. My mother still has the picture of my graduation ceremony. I'm standing in the middle, all dressed up in a white suit with a carnation in the lapel, smiling my crooked smile.

About that time, our family also had a rather unusual ceremony, the "shoes celebration." We had a family party with a cake, chairs gathered around the table, and lots of laughter. My dad even composed a song for the occasion. I don't remember much about it, except that it contained the words "heels and toes," which was appropriate because we were celebrating the fact that, for the first time, I had worn out a shoe on the bottom. There was actually wear that you could measure on the heels of my shoes! Before then, I pulled the tops off the toes of my shoes because I dragged my feet so badly.

After I had successfully navigated the dangerous waters of kindergarten, I was ready for "real school"—first grade. First grade brought big changes in my life. In school and at home I had to take speech therapy two or three times a week. I remember how happy I was when I escaped the k's: kay, key, kai, koe, koo. But I stayed for quite a while with the s's: see, sight, saw, so, sue. For years, I had to have speech therapy and special tutoring in reading and math after school. Writing was and still is a challenge for me. It caused me to fail two half grades in elementary school.

In spite of my difficulties, Miss Wills said, "Absolutely not!" when my teachers wanted to put me in the "opportunity class." This was a class for slow learners. Miss Wills refused, and when they persisted, she said, "Your challenge is to meet the needs of this youngster . . . or else!"

She also appointed me as a safety patrolman. Only somebody who cared for me like Miss Wills, considering my lack of coordination, slowness of foot and poor motor skills, would select me as one of the young men to lead the school to safety, peradventure the place would burn. Thank God, there was no fire.

My lack of coordination and poor motor skills didn't prevent me from participating in a schoolyard track meet. I went out for every event. The dash, broad jump . . . can you imagine? I barely got in from one race in time to start the second. The long jump—I got all my stride spaces just right—and full speed ahead hit the board, flung myself in the air, and barely made it to the front edge of the pit. But, so what? I was involved. The high jump was really something. I took my three shots at the low mark and missed. For some reason (I suppose it was wisdom) they wouldn't allow me to take part in the pole-vaulting event.

Several weeks after the track meet, an assembly was called, where the trophies and medals were given out. All of a sudden Miss Wills called my name. The students stomped and clapped and whistled and she pinned a little medal on my shirt. The place went into total pandemonium. I don't know if I walked down the steps or floated back to my seat. A couple of weeks later I started thinking, *I got a medal but what event did I win?* I went to my dresser, found the medal and looked at it, and it said, "Congratulations." That's it, just "Congratulations." Of course, now I realize that they were saying, "We admire and respect you, and first of all we love you."

Although I loved to play sports, I was never very good. When the neighborhood kids would choose sides for a game of sandlot softball, I would be the last one chosen. I'd stand off to the side, my hands in my pockets and my head down. I'd scuff circles in the dirt, while the two captains fought over who had to take me. "You take him. O no, I had him last time." I tried to act casual, but inside I felt humiliated and hurt. The only time I wasn't chosen last was when my best friend, John Cupit, was playing. Cupit was such an outstanding athlete, everybody wanted him on their team, and it was understood that whoever took Cupit got me in the bargain.

Cupit usually pitched, and I would catch for him. I could catch because you could do that with just one good hand—and no one else wanted the position. It was too easy to get hurt! But even at catcher, my skills were limited. I could barely get the ball back to the pitcher, and if we played by hardball rules, which allowed a runner to steal second, I couldn't throw to second.

Cupit's friendship got me on the team, but once there, I was on my own. He wouldn't protect me. One day he was catching and for some reason, I was on the other team. By some miracle, I had gotten a base hit and was on first base, feeling my oats. If anyone knew my weaknesses, it was Cupit. He knew that if I got to first, I would show off, and I did, taking too big a lead off the base. Lo and behold, Cupit threw me out at first. It's been forty years, but I still haven't forgiven him.

In spite of my obvious deficiencies, it never occurred to me that I couldn't play ball because I was handicapped. I just thought I wasn't good enough. It hurt to want so bad to be good and not to be, but I never stopped trying. I may have struck out or been thrown out before I got to first base, but I never considered not going to bat.

I'm certain things would have been different if I had known I was crippled. I don't think I would have kept on competing if I had realized that no matter how hard I tried, I was never going to be able to make it.

Looking back at those early years, I have often wondered how my parents managed to prevent me from discovering my handicap. I think they must have engaged the entire neighborhood in a conspiracy to protect me.

Of course, in the 1930s and '40s, a child's world was considerably smaller than it is today. There was much less mobility. Few families had more than one car. Suburbs and shopping malls were unknown and the freeways and beltways around major cities, so common today, were rare. Children walked to neighborhood schools. Although New Orleans was a major port city, each of its four principal areas was divided into dozens of smaller "neighborhoods"—tiny, self-contained communities. Each neighborhood had its own churches, schools and a shopping area. Shopping areas were usually one or two streets long with a grocery store, pharmacy, bakery, clothing store, laundry and dry cleaners, shoe repair shop, garage, barber shop—and maybe a movie theatre.

Our extended neighborhood may have been as large as thirteen blocks, but the boundaries of my world were much smaller. Its perimeter was Tchoupitoulas Street between Bellcastle and Dufossat—about two or three blocks.

We lived at 5219 Tchoupitoulas Street. Shortly after I was born, my parents had been evicted from the house on Perrier Street, for failing to pay the rent. Perrier ran through an old, affluent part of New Orleans. Being forced to move to Tchoupitoulas Street presented a noticeable decline in our fortunes. Bounded on the riverside by the railroad tracks, it was a lower middle class neighborhood at best.

We rented a yellow, wood-framed, shotgun house with four rooms and a bath, separated from its neighbors on both sides by a wooden fence. At one end of the street was a Shell station, which my dad had helped to build, and at the other was Drobe's Grocery Store.

Across the street were more shotgun houses like ours. At the end of the block, around the corner, was a large house, where the local ward boss lived. He liked to lean out of his window and toss coins for the neighborhood kids to fight over. Behind his house was a bar and dance hall, which was used for school and neighborhood dances and socials. This was bordered by the railroad tracks and a vacant lot where we played ball. On the other side of the tracks was a grain elevator and the New Orleans furniture factory. I wasn't allowed to go across the tracks.

Two blocks toward Canal Street on Tchoupitoulas Street was a stable where they kept the horses that pulled the trash wagons. Every evening, when I heard the steady clop, clop, clop of their hooves on the pavement, I would stop whatever I was doing and rush to the pavement to watch the long, slow procession of these sad-eyed beasts as they made their way back to the stable.

Evenings were a special time. There was no air conditioning or TV, so on spring and summer nights the neighborhood would be dotted with porch gatherings. Everybody would sit with three or four friends on somebody's porch, drink their beer or root beer, and swap gossip, while the kids played in the street, or down the sidewalks. Everyone knew everything about everybody in that little world.

During the war, I worked after school at Drobe's store, selling penny candy. I was paid one defense stamp a week. Just outside the store, there was an eight-inch-wide beam, about twenty feet long, which sat on blocks along one side of the building. The furniture factory workers would buy sandwiches in Drobe's, then sit on the bench to eat them. Because labor was scarce, the government had sent Japanese P.O.W.'s to work in the factory. When the trucks carrying them to and from work passed Drobe's, the men would get up off the bench and throw bricks at them.

The day the war ended, I was walking back from school and heard the news over a radio through an open window. I raced home to find everyone poured out into the streets, shouting, singing, and crying. In the midst of the general chaos, I was frustrated because everyone else had a noisemaker and I couldn't find one. I finally ended up banging two railroad spikes together.

I have nothing but happy memories of those days. I was never aware of the kids in the neighborhood making fun of or being sarcastic to me. The closest thing to come to that was never being picked first. I had lots of friends and I can't remember one time when anyone was cruel to me. Either my parents had done a very good job in convincing everyone to treat me normally, or I was very naïve, but I never received anything but respect and care from anyone in that neighborhood. In fact, of all the places I've lived throughout my life, no place has held the charm of Tchoupitoulas Street.

The family, 1953—Dad, Mom, Sonny and me

3

Family Ties

WITHOUT QUESTION, THE BIGGEST influence in my young life was my family.

My mother ran our home and our lives with a sometimes ruthless efficiency. She was a vigorous, large woman (always 50–100 pounds overweight), with a sharp, no-nonsense approach to life. A strong will beamed in her clear green eyes. It was impossible to mistake her meaning—she was forthright and direct.

As a young woman she had been something of a free spirit. She rebelled against the misery of her home and determined to find some joy in life. She loved music, and before she came into the church, she was quite a good dancer. One night she was attending a dance at the Octavia Street Dance Hall, when a Salvation Army girl came in. Threading her way through the dancing couples, she reached my mother and asked, "Sister, couldn't you spare just a quarter for Jesus?" That shook up my mother so badly, she left the dance, and shortly afterward got her life straightened out with God. From my boyish perspective, it was hard to imagine that my devoutly Pentecostal mother had ever entered a dance hall!

Although we were often short of money during most of my childhood, she did not take a job outside the home. She volunteered for the Community Chest, and did bookkeeping for the church. She was also active in the P.T.A. and occasionally prodded my father into constructing booths for the school carnival.

My mother was the chief disciplinarian in our home. She had a hot temper and was quick with a jab. Transgressions were often rewarded with a swift, stinging swat, and my handicap didn't prevent me from receiving my share. In this approach to discipline, she and my father differed. He was reluctant to use force, although she sometimes badgered him to "take care of the boys." Our parents presented a largely united front to my brother and me, but occasionally their disagreement flared openly. One night my mother backhanded me for something I had done at the dinner table. My father didn't say anything, but he put his coffee cup down with unusual emphasis. Not one for subtleties, my mother reached over, picked up his cup and slammed it down again, so that the coffee flew all over the room.

Although my father also had an explosive temper, he only whipped me once. I had gone across the tracks and down to the levee where I had somehow borrowed a horse and ridden way down behind Audubon Park, which was twenty-five blocks away. I was just having fun, but my parents panicked when they couldn't find me, walking the entire twenty-five blocks, questioning people who might have seen me. I don't remember if they found me or if I finally just came home on my own, but I do remember my dad beating me with his belt. Even then, however, he felt bad when it was all over and gave me a quarter.

For most of my childhood, my grandmother VanHorssen lived with us, which gave my mother a built-in babysitter. My grandmother was even larger than my mother, but then grandmothers were supposed to be big and soft. She was a real prayer warrior. Because she couldn't kneel, she would sit in her big rocking chair, rocking and praying. I heard her pray for me every night. She'd pray over and over that the Lord would call me to preach. "Give him an appealing ministry, Lord," she prayed. When I got older and started to preach, that word became a part of my prayer. I asked for a ministry that would not be appeasing, but appealing. When I was evangelizing, I knew that no matter where I was, from eight to nine that night she'd be praying. I knew that when I walked to the pulpit she would still be asking God for an appealing ministry for me, and that was very strengthening.

Although they loved me deeply, my mother and grandmother leaned a little in their preference toward my brother Sonny.

Sonny and I were not very close. For a long time I blamed that on the fact that we were five years apart, but I have met other brothers who were five years apart and were very close. It was not age, but interests, which separated us. We simply did not have much in common. I loved sports, he disliked them. I liked getting dirty, he liked being clean. I could have cared less what clothes I wore (until I became interested in girls!), he was very careful about the way he dressed. He liked school, I liked recess.

As long as we went to the same school, my parents made him walk me there and back each day. I'm certain he must have resented having to care for his rowdy pest of a brother instead of walking with his friends. But occasionally he got revenge. I still walked slowly, and one day when he was in a hurry to get home, he grew impatient. He picked a red berry off a bush at the corner of Annunciation and Jefferson Ave. "Hey, Allan, try this," he said. "You'll like it. It tastes like candy." I believed him, until I popped it in my mouth and discovered it was a hot pepper. I ran the rest of the way home.

My brother disliked conflict of any kind and never got into the kind of schoolyard scrapes that other boys did—except once. The neighborhood bully had been harassing me.

It didn't take much to upset my already precarious balance, so he would wait for me at the end of the street, push me over, then laugh as my arms and legs flailed wildly in every direction on my way down to the sidewalk. After several days of this, my brother got wind of it and came to my defense. The bully was not so tough when faced with someone his own size and strength and Sonny whipped him soundly. For days after that, he was my hero. Oddly enough, at the time I never connected the fact that the bully picked on me with my being handicapped. I still didn't know I was. I just knew that Sonny had scored a great victory over my tormentor.

If Sonny was favored by my mother and grandmother, there was no doubt that I was my daddy's boy.

My father was tall and lanky, with the same long, skinny arms as my grandfather. Neither of them had much of a bicep, but they were strong. They explained this mystery to me by saying that because their arms were so long, the muscle extension from the shoulder to the elbow was longer, which prevented them from having big biceps. I believed it then.

I adored my dad. To me, he was the strongest, handsomest man in the world. Although my physical limitations were in great contrast to his strength, I was never envious or resentful. I felt like, "You have it, and you're mine."

More than anything else in life I wanted his approval. But I seldom got it. Although he showed his love in a thousand unspoken ways, it was difficult for him to express love or pride in words. I think my drive to succeed originated in my relationship with my dad. I would have done anything to receive an expression of praise from him. It was my biggest "want-to." Although, as I got older, I used that desire in the pursuit of other goals, I think in my heart I was still pursuing my dad's praise.

Even when times were difficult, my dad always worked. He was a carpenter by trade and an excellent craftsman. Once he did some carpentry work for a chiropractor and in return, the doctor made some adjustments on me. My dad belonged to the local carpenter's union and usually worked wherever they sent him. But once he started his own business—Theodore A. Oggs Construction Co. He had a big old paneled truck with his name written on the side in script. He did mostly remodeling work, and his business venture only lasted about a year.

Sometimes I would fake being sick so I wouldn't have to go to school. He would come by the house about 9 A.M. to check on me, and suddenly I would get better. Then I'd go out with him and watch him work. He was a good workman, dexterous, and when he was happy and the job was going well, he'd sing or whistle hymns.

Even when he worked, he was careful to shield me from the knowledge of my handicap. When he painted a wall, he put the hand that wasn't holding a brush in his pocket. I had to do that in order to anchor my bad arm, and for years I thought that everybody painted one-handed.

During my first eleven years, my dad received the Holy Ghost, backslid, then prayed through again. During the time when he was backslidden, he worked for a while as a night bartender in a sandwich shop on Bellcastle. I wasn't allowed to cross Bellcastle Street, so I would sit in a little drainage ditch on my side, just to catch a glimpse of him when someone opened the door. Forty years later, I still buy my sandwiches at Domilise's when I'm in town.

My father was a gregarious, sociable person. He loved a party. In New Orleans, each neighborhood had its own neighborhood social club. At Mardi Gras, the members would dress up in costumes and parade through the streets. Our neighborhood club was the Jefferson City Buzzards. They had their own marching jazz band and my dad joined in as a marching Buzzard. I can remember him carrying a coffee can in the parade, but I knew the can didn't contain coffee—it contained beer. The Buzzards would dance and strut through the streets, pausing at designated stops along the way—all the bars, where they could get free beer. Of course, when he came back into the church, that clipped his wings.

But re-joining the church didn't dampen his sense of humor. My dad loved a good joke and had a boisterous laugh. After he died, a church he had once pastored was sold. When the new owners went in to renovate and began tearing out walls, they found cartoons that my dad had drawn on the inside of the walls. He was always doodling or drawing portraits of people and actually he was a pretty good artist.

When I was six, my dad was offered an opportunity to join a group of civilian workers who were going to Panama to help refurbish the Canal. I went down to the docks with my mother to see him off. It was 1941, and in spite of its declared neutrality, the United States was obviously beginning to prepare for war. In addition to the usual tugs, steamers, and huge coal barges, the harbor was clogged with naval ships, great gray behemoths, bristling with weapons. My dad boarded one of these. Tanks were lined end to end on the deck, covered with tarpaulins. I was so fascinated by all the activity, I almost forgot how devastated I was that my dad was going away. We watched the ship pull away from the dock and waved until it was out of sight. But, when I turned to go home with my mother, I felt an inconsolable sense of loss.

My dad was in Panama for only six months. World War II intervened, and all the civilian workers were sent home. Dad told my mother that on the way back, his ship had to use the exercises it had practiced for avoiding submarines. He loved Panama, and if the war hadn't broken out, he would have stayed. He had arranged a government job for my mother and we were going to join him. I think they planned to work a few years, build a nice nest egg, and come home.

The day he came home, I was next door. I saw a cab pull to the curb and my dad get out. The house I was visiting was surrounded by a wire fence. Instead of going out the gate, I thought I would show my dad how much I had improved, so I tried to climb over the fence. He hadn't seen my mom in six months and all the excitement of seeing her again, touching her, had to stop while they watched me climb the fence. I had no problem getting to the top, but then I couldn't get down. I was stuck. He had to leave her arms to come over and get me.

Having my dad home was like Christmas, my birthday and the Fourth of July all rolled into one. But my happiness was marred slightly when he opened his footlocker and a carton of Lucky Strikes fell out. Although I was only seven, I knew cigarette-smoking was a sin, and having Lucky Strikes in his footlocker meant he was still away from God.

The night he prayed through again, I made the altar before he did. Our church was having a revival and the preacher's name was Mason Starks. I was so excited when I heard my daddy praying. When he began to praise the Lord, I knew everything was all right.

After my dad came back to God, our whole lives revolved around the church. The revival that brought my folks into the church was a neighborhood affair. Now you can have a revival and your converts may come from thirty-five miles away. In this case, however, most of the converts came from the neighborhood. You could walk to church and gather people along the way.

The church was on Octavia Street, just around the corner from where the original tent had stood. There was a fish market at the end of the street which smelled terrible. For years church was associated with a slightly fishy odor in my mind. But across the street, there was a bakery and the wonderful aroma of fresh baked breads and pastries, which emanated from it, almost compensated for the fish. After church, while the adults fellowshipped, we kids would go to the bakery to watch Mr. Rappo bake bread. He would let us dip a finger into the chocolate and strawberry icings.

The church was small and badly needed talent. Normally in a UPC church, you don't hold any offices or take a leading role in the service for a while, but my dad began playing his banjo immediately. Before long, he had held every office in the church, which sometimes created problems for me. One Sunday morning I had been expelled from my Sunday school class for teasing the girls. Standing out in the hall, I begged to be let back inside. My dad was Superintendent of the Sunday school then and I was terrified he would decide to make his rounds before I could get back in. I knew there would be big trouble if he found me standing outside in the hallway.

My grandfather had the distinction of hanging every door in the church and the Sunday school rooms. Today, you buy prehung doors, but it was quite a job then. You have to be a good carpenter to hang a door. My grandparents and John Cupit's parents were charter members of that church. Today, John Cupit is the pastor and my son is interning there. My grandson Clint is the fifth generation Oggs in that church.

Not long after I was born, J. B. Thomas married John Cupit's sister. She was fifteen years younger than Pastor Thomas, but she was about thirteen years older than Cupit. So when they got married, it was almost as if John Cupit was his son. Brother Thomas was like a dad to Cupit. He took Cupit and his friend, me, all over the country to conventions and rallies. We all stayed in the same room, and all I had to do was to pay my share. I can still recall sister Ailene Thomas in her slip.

I was a grown man when Brother Thomas died. He had prayed for me in the hospital, and baptized me in the name of the Lord Jesus Christ the night I received the Holy Ghost. We both lived long enough for me to preach for him, so we were very close. Sister Thomas has long since remarried, but she is very fond of reminding me about those times we had together.

When I was eleven, we moved to Phoenix, Arizona. At the time, my dad was operating a laundry route and doing a little preaching on the side. My grandma Nellie had a half-brother who lived in Arizona. He owned some of the waterworks and a Studebaker dealership in Phoenix. On a trip to New Orleans, he encouraged my dad to come back with him to Arizona. The offer was, "Come on out, and we'll put together a cleaning plant and help you start a church."

As it turned out, there were a lot of problems. Grandma's half-brother and his family were Methodists and my folks were

Pentecostal; they were socialites, my folks were working people; they had money, my folks had none. So we stayed about six months. When we left we had to sell almost everything we owned to get enough money to get back home. We came back from Arizona with three big barrels of pots and pans, clothing and some sparse household furnishings. That was the measure of all my daddy's possessions. He lost everything except what was in those barrels, and somebody broke into one of them on the way home.

When we got home, we moved in with his sister, Viola. She had been married so often that most lost count, but she loved her brother and would have done anything for him. In fact, it was her current "boarder" who loaned my dad enough money to make a down payment on a house.

Pop Murrell was his name and he was a colorful character. He was a gambler from New York and he'd come to Louisiana every year following the horse races. Oh, he had some stories. He claimed to have traveled with the circus and to have been a tour guide in New York City. He may have been my aunt's boarder, but he was good to me.

Our first Christmas home he bought me a Lionel train set. That was a big deal in those days. At the time, we didn't have any living or dining room furniture. Anyone could tell we were broke, but there I was with one of the best train sets money could buy.

Our new house was on Arabella Street. The Arabella house was one half block from the beginning of a well-to-do neighborhood. We got that close. We had no car, but my dad did some painting at night for the Fairchild Motor Co. and they gave him a three-wheel motorcycle, so that's what we used for travel. When I rode on the back of the motorcycle, I thought I was sure enough downtown.

Our new house was in a different school district. Instead of the old, familiar Daniel School, I had to go to McDonald 14 School and I was scared. The only thing that made it a little easier was that Miss Wills had moved to McDonald 14 too.

Also, I could walk from McDonald 14 to my grandma's to eat lunch with my dad. It was about six blocks but I had an hour. Sometimes my dad would drive me back to school.

My grandmother Nellie had a large old house with two apartments upstairs which she rented out. She always seemed to have someone living upstairs. Usually it was someone from the church who needed a place to stay temporarily, but it was never a stranger. The renters did their own cooking and everything. I can't recall ever being upstairs. It was like having two separate houses.

I don't remember my brother ever going with me to lunch at my grandmother's. That's not surprising, however. Just as my mother and her family were partial to Sonny, my father and his family favored me. I doubt that knowing we were favored by one side of the family or the other ever bothered either of us. There was enough love to go around, and we knew that as diverse as our family was, it also maintained an essential unity. We had no doubts about the importance of Family.

The move to Arabella Street effectively ended my childhood. I was heading into adolescence and would soon experience a traumatic encounter that would alter the way I looked at myself and at life. But the love and support I received from my family in those early years gave me a security that none of the storms of life have ever been able to destroy.

4

The End of Innocence

FRITZI AND I GOT INTO a fight and I swung but missed; I couldn't hit him. So I stuck out my chin and said, "Hit me."

"I can't," he said.

"I know you can't because you're scared," I taunted him.

"I'm not scared. I can't hit you because you're a cripple."

In an instant, I said, "You're right."

All those years of spilled water, the stumbling, the things I had done that meant nothing to me—suddenly, it all made sense. And as suddenly, I was devastated.

I ran home and headed straight for my bedroom, slammed the door, but forgot to lock it. Then I hit bottom. I cried to myself, "Nobody loves me. The girls won't ever like me and those who act like they do now are just feeling sorry for me." I was feeling so sorry for myself. I just knew there was no future for me. I was crushed.

Then my mom came in—big, strong and heavy. She sat

on the edge of the bed, tilting the whole thing. She didn't shed one tear, and she didn't touch me with her hand. But with her wit, her wisdom and her words she beat me to a pulp. She splattered me on the wall.

"Don't you ever feel sorry for yourself!" she said. "You are somebody and you have a lot of people who love you. Do you think your father would have spent hours every day teaching you to walk and to play ball, if he didn't care? Do you think we would have hired all those speech therapists and tutors if we didn't love you? Do you think Cupit just pretends to be your friend because he feels sorry for you? You know better than that! Cupit loves you like a brother. And what about Miss Wills? Those people believe in you. You can do anything you want to in life!"

When she finished, she got up, the bed leveled off and she went to the door. Without a tear, she looked back and screamed, "*As long as you live, don't you ever forget what I told you!*" I learned years later that after she left my room, she went to hers, and came unglued. But she knew I didn't need that. I needed some muscle.

It seemed like everything had been moving toward a slot and then it fell in place. When it did, it all made sense. And when I say everything, I mean everything. You've heard of a dying man seeing his life flash before him—that's what happened to me. I saw everything. I felt naked. I wasn't ignorant. I wasn't a dummy. I don't know what I thought before when I fell or spilled the water, except that it must not have been devastating, embarrassing or humiliating. It was just "oops." But after that it wasn't just "oops" because I knew why.

This new awareness of my physical problems created psychological and social difficulties. First it was the Prytania Theatre. I was twelve years old, living in the home of a Pentecostal preacher, and I had never been to a movie. One Friday night when I was supposed to be going to a Scout meeting, I jumped on my bicycle and instead of going to the meeting, I went to a neighborhood theatre, the Prytania.

I bought a ticket. Then I went inside, and sat down rather awkwardly, thinking that if they didn't turn the lights out soon everybody would know I was there. I sat and wiggled and squirmed and prayed for the lights to go off. Finally the lights began to dim and darkness came. Now, my deeds were evil and it was real dark, so I should have felt right at home. Ah! darkness . . . I'm in the right place. When the lights went out I thought, *Now this is my time to really enjoy myself.*

Little did I know that when the lights went out, it was the signal for my conscience, the greatest preacher on earth, to walk to my "inside pulpit," grab his Bible and start preaching. "You have no business here, you are supposed to be at Scout meeting." What would happen if the place burned down, and all they would find would be my little red bicycle, hidden in the alley? The message was so strong that I thought I smelled smoke. I jumped up and went out and told the manager, "I want out of here! Give me my money back!"

The manager told me I could leave any time I wished, but they only returned money to those who were real sick. I said, "Lady, take a real good look at me. You don't realize it, but I am really sick. There is something on the inside of me, that if it ever bursts, I'm liable to die right here." I got my money and away I went.

The Prytania theatre incident was the beginning of my life of "crime." While I was struggling to adjust to who and what I was, I got into all kinds of trouble—drinking, smoking, cussing, getting kicked out of school, even shoplifting.

There was the time I came home with a beautiful white plastic football helmet. Brand new! I told my dad that the high school had purchased new ones and threw these "old things" away. One glance at his face told me he knew I was lying. He gathered up about $500 worth of football equipment that I and a few friends had stolen, took it back to the coach and made things right.

I wasn't even a very smart crook. When my friends and I would go shoplifting the other guys would try to be sneaky.

Not me. I'd brag, "Watch me," snatch the stuff off the shelves and openly walk out the door. I got kicked out of school a lot, just for talking and being unruly. The other kids would cut up and stop when the teacher came in, but I kept on.

I wanted to lead. I made an honest attempt in some areas to lead, but how could I? I always brought up the rear. But I could be the class clown and everyone would laugh and love it.

In many ways I was not as bad as I liked to pretend, however. Take smoking for example. I never learned to inhale, because I almost choked to death every time I tried. But I bought my pack and stuck it in my pocket. I did the same thing with cigars. I doubt if I drank any real amount of alcohol, either, but I'd sip enough to smell like I did and I'd flop around and act silly, as if I wanted to fight and all that kind of stuff.

I wanted so desperately to be a leader, to be noticed, to be a part of the crowd, that I would do almost anything. But one of my exploits almost got me in serious trouble.

One day I crawled through a neighbor's window and carried away a bunch of knick-knacks. They weren't very valuable, but legally I was guilty of breaking and entering. The police came to school, took me out of class, sat me in the principal's office and were about to formally charge me, when Miss Wills asked to talk to the officers alone. I don't know what she said, but the officer took me home and said if no one pressed charges, maybe I had learned my lesson.

A few days later I was sitting in the kitchen, the back room of our big, long, shotgun house, and there was a knock at the front door. My dad walked from the kitchen all the way through three bedrooms, dining room, living room (known in New Orleans as the "front room"), opened the door and there stood a uniformed policeman. I'll never forget what followed.

The officer explained to my dad what I had done, and my dad, the man who meant so very much to me, looked across the kitchen table at me, and began to cry silently. I thought, *Dad, please don't cry. Slap me, punch me, but please don't cry.* His shoulders shook, his belly quivered, his face got all squeezed into an awkward shape. No tears, but he cried, and he said to me, "My God, son, how could you do this after all the Lord has done for you?"

The officer explained that the lady who owned the house was pressing charges and dropped her name. When he did, my father spoke up and said, "Officer, are you sure that's whose house it was?" He said "Yes," and my dad said, "Give me two hours and I'll take care of it." As it turned out, the lady was having an extramarital affair and my dad happened to know about it. A few remarks to her concerning his knowledge and she was quite eager to help the youngster who made a mistake by dropping all charges. My dad told me, "I'm going to get you back in school, but it is the last time."

I loved my parents so much and I knew what I was doing was hurting them. I felt tremendous guilt not only for doing wrong before God, but also because my dad was just starting his ministry and here I was stealing, cussing, smoking cigars, and getting kicked out of school. I didn't want to hurt anybody, but I was so confused. Fortunately, God intervened in time to protect me from myself. It happened right in the middle of my most rebellious time.

My parents made me go to church on Sunday, but I didn't have to go during the week. However, one Thursday night I decided to go to church with my dad. The preacher that evening supposedly had been in prison, and I thought he would have a good story. As it turned out, his story was all fraud. He probably should have gone to jail, but he never had. I walked to church with my dad that night and passed all the houses I had been stealing from. It was May 3, 1951.

Right before the preacher gave the altar call, I remember thinking, *I am so confused, if God could somehow clear my head, then we would have a deal. If living for him would end my confusion, I'd do it.* And that's exactly what happened. While I was trying to describe in prayer what I hoped would occur, all of a sudden it did. The clearness, the release that I had hoped to earn, suddenly it was there—a gift of God. I felt clean, I felt relief. I felt release. Then when I began to express my joy for what had happened, what I was saying was not in English. I was speaking in tongues, a language I had never learned. My dad, standing a good fifteen or so feet from me, was so pleased that he lifted his long arms toward the ceiling and at the top of his voice (it seemed like the very ceiling vibrated), he shouted, "Hallelujah!"

The experience was so real. It was not just in my head. I could actually feel the Lord come into my life. I had thought that I would never smile again when I became a Christian. I thought it would be a solemn, sober experience, but from minute one I had a smile from ear to ear. It didn't clear up all my problems for life, but I felt immediately like, "Hey, come on. I know who You are. I know who I am, I know where I come from, and I have a ways to go, but I know where I am going!"

My mom was not at church that night. When I got home I wanted to tell her face to face but she was in the bathroom, so I called, "Mama, come out." Usually my request meant that I wanted in the bathroom so she said, "Wait your turn."

By then it was midnight and I called a friend and woke him up to tell him what had happened, too. I couldn't understand why he wasn't as excited as I.

During the next few weeks, the guys who had always been my pals told me they didn't want to be friends with me anymore. Of course, after I received the Holy Ghost, I didn't want to continue doing what I had been doing, so that was fine. I always had friends at the church and they were there if I wanted them.

I couldn't have received the Holy Ghost at a better time. I graduated from grammar school that same month and then we moved to Kenner, a suburb of New Orleans where my dad was starting a church. By the time I got to Kenner, I was just the preacher's son. As far as they knew, I had nothing to live down, nothing to pull away from.

"Behold, all things (did) become new," and almost too fast! There was a new Christian walk, a new city, a new school and a new church. I was sixteen years old that September, old enough to realize that "no one can do everything," and I was scared. No more friends such as Fritzi, no more McDonald 14 School. Miss Wills was gone and so was the cozy, comfortable feeling of my neighborhood with all its unique and wonderful people. I was cast out of my protected nest.

I call this my "preacher's suit" (early 1951)

The conqueror of Kenner High, 1955

5

"You Want to Do What?"

KENNER HIGH BECAME for me an experience, perhaps *the* experience of a lifetime. It threw a coming out party that was hosted by a team of compassionate, professional specialists. God must have trained them for years, preparing them to handle me. It was hands-on from day one.

Those first few days of class were something. All the other kids had been together from the first grade. I was determined to find my place somewhere, or if not, "I wasn't going to be pushed around."

My history class was still in the "sign-your-name-on-the-sheet" stage, when I got acquainted with the teacher, Mrs. Largesse, "head-on." I don't remember what she said, but I made some smart remark to the kids sitting next to me and she heard it. She thundered, "Who said that?"

I was shaken to my toes. I said, "I did."

"And who are you?"

After I told her, she said, "The next time you do that, you will pick yourself up out in the hall after hitting the lockers."

That was my introduction to Mrs. Largesse, who was to become a tremendous blessing to my life. Later, I had a confrontation with her of a different sort. She made a statement in history class that "the book of Job in the Old Testament is a parable." I was still scared of her because she was so aggressive and strong-willed, but I couldn't let that pass. Gathering up my courage, I spoke up.

"Mrs. Largesse, you do not have the right to mislead these pupils with that kind of statement."

She just glared at me and said nothing. The bell rang, and class was dismissed. She asked me to stay behind, and I thought surely this would be my assassination. When I approached her desk she asked me, "I have noticed in the local newspaper that there is a Rev. Theodore Oggs, Jr., pastor of the new First Pentecostal Church here in Kenner. Is that your father?"

I said, "Yes."

She said, "Thank you, you may go now."

The next four years, I took every history course the school offered. She never answered another question that had anything to do with religion. Instead, she would field the question and then throw it to me. I would do the very best I could to answer it from a purely Sunday school background. Mrs. Largesse will always be a fond memory in my life.

Another colorful character who made an impact on my life was Joe Yenni, our state champion football coach. Yenni was competitive, hard and at times, just plain mean. He had a temper that would make him bite his tongue and burn his face.

I really became acquainted with Joseph Yenni about the second week of school. Our physical education class was co-ed. I had a religious scruple concerning wearing shorts in mixed company and now it was countdown time. Coach Yenni announced, "You who do not have your gym shorts remain, and the rest of you go to the football field."

About half a dozen of us stayed behind. I was scared

beyond words. I had seen this man drop-kick a 200-pound plus tackle in the seat of his pants. I knew what he could do. Down the line he came.

"Where are your shorts?" And there was a reason, an excuse, a promise; the next one would say the same. Finally it was my turn to be blasted.

"Where are your shorts? And when will you have them?"

I said, "Mr. Yenni, I do not have any shorts and I'm not going to get any."

Everybody ought to know Joe Yenni, because knowing him adds something to living. He got in my face, almost nose-to-nose, with nostrils flaring, teeth showing, his tongue stuck out while he chewed it, and said, "*What?*"

I explained that, because of a religious scruple, I could not wear shorts in mixed company. He said, "Are you trying to goldbrick on me?"

I said, "No, sir; if anybody likes to play, I do. And whatever you require the other students to do, I'll do my best to do it . . . but in long pants." He began that morning to stack something very important inside of me.

"If you think you're going to goldbrick around me, get special privileges, you are all wrong. You 'sit' on me and I'll run you up and down that field until your tongue hangs to your knee caps."

"Yes, sir."

One day in p.e. class, we were divided into two groups for a touch football game. I'm not talking eleven on eleven but a class divided in two, about thirty-five on each side. And we had to play on the sidelines because the main field was being prepared for an up-coming game. So instead of being fifty-five feet wide, the field was twenty-five feet wide, and instead of having eleven opponents, we had thirty-five.

Now, there was an understood rule that if the ball came to me I was supposed to get out of the way and not touch it. But on this particular day the ball came right at me. Either I had to catch it or I would eat it, so I caught it. I wasn't supposed to run either, because I was a liability, but I ran! I ran the whole eighty yards . . . everybody who got close to me flipped, tripped, stumbled or fell. I got all pumped up and excited. I thought I was Mr. "Crazy-legs" himself; I was gone. Nobody laid a hand on me, and I scored a touchdown.

A few days later I got to thinking, *That can't be possible, thirty-five men coming at me, spread across a meager twenty-five yards width, and I'm running in slow motion. Ain't no way.* Joe Yenni and seventy fine young men conspired to produce for me a special day. I've not seen Joe Yenni in years; I've corresponded with him, and these many years later, I still love, respect and admire him. He is now the parish president of Jefferson Parish in the greater New Orleans Metropolitan area.

I got my first job while in high school, fixing flats, changing oil and pumping gas, at an Esso station. On my first day, the owner, Bob Mitchell, said, "I want you to meet your boss, Robbie." So Robbie came out, a small fellow. I was scared to death. Then Robbie smiled and stuck out his left hand. His right hand was totally gone and on his left he had no thumb and could only bend his fingers a little. I thought, *Wow, look at this guy, he's worse off than I am.*

Who would have thought that my first job would be so physical? To check the oil I had to use two hands, and I had to hug the tires to change them. I stayed filthy dirty, but I did everything they told me. After a few weeks, I was feeling like a real man. I had staked out this job and conquered it. Then I discovered that my dad had gotten the job for me. That really deflated my ego.

From there I went to work with a company that my dad was working for as a carpenter's helper. I was what they call a "butterer." Now they suspend ceilings on a metal grid. Then, they stuck the ceiling tile to the old ceiling. You would put a glob of glue (they called it butter) at the four corners of the tile. Can you imagine with my coordination? I had glue all over me, but I did it.

My next job was at a supermarket. Cupit worked there

also. They had thirty-two checkout stands and about twenty bag boys. We worked on tips. We had an unending contest to see who could make the most. I never placed less than third. That meant a lot to me. I hustled, but looking back, I think I may have had an edge because I was handicapped. But, there again, I wasn't aware of anybody laughing or making fun.

As we got older, Cupit and I ran a little lawn service business. He was the muscle, and did most of the mowing. I went to the door and got business—and kept track of our finances. I did my fair share of the work, but he didn't like doing the negotiating.

I had two social worlds—my school friends and my church friends. Neither group resented the other and both groups respected me. My church doesn't believe in dancing, movies, and things like that, so I couldn't do much socializing with my school friends on the weekend. But they understood that. It was just part of life. When Friday came, it was "see you Monday." Saturday and Sunday I'd be involved either with my dad's little church in Kenner, or with the young people in the church in New Orleans.

As much as I was loved in high school and as many friends as I had, I was still self-conscious about certain aspects of my handicap. In the four years I was at Kenner High, I never put my foot inside the school lunchroom. I couldn't carry my tray from the cafeteria line to the table, and I didn't want to ask for help. So I ate sandwiches on the corners of the school ground. That was silly. Anybody there would have been glad to carry my tray. They knew my handicap like the back of their hands, but that was something I never did face in high school.

I don't know why I was so shy about asking for assistance. I can't remember ever being refused help. However, I've never felt that people were supposed to do anything for me. I've mentioned to my kids many times that I've received a lot of love they never will, because I'm crippled. Total strangers, people I'll never see twice, have been kind to me. And I needed it sometimes.

Of course, there is another side to that. Sometimes I received help I didn't need or want. Sometimes people have embarrassed me, but I've never said anything. I knew they were sincerely concerned and to say "buzz off" would have been terrible.

I still can't carry a plate in a cafeteria, but now I don't hesitate to ask for help. However, I have learned that if you ask people to carry your tray, they want to cut your meat and butter your bread as well! So, I always say, "I only have problems from the counter to the table." And I laugh and add, "I'm sure it's obvious to you that I have no problems from the plate to the lip."

I think a lot of the negatives that some handicapped people live with are brought on by themselves. I have been very blessed in that I have always had people who encouraged me to use what I had. I don't think I have a whole lot of anything. But, a whole army of people have said to me in word or action, "If you're going to hang around with me, if you are an 80 or 50 or 90 percent, use the 90 and I'll give you the 10. But if you are a 90 and you are only going to use 50, don't think I'm going to give you 50."

What I lacked people were always willing to compensate for, but only what I really lacked. And I don't think I asked for more.

When I became a sophomore in high school, I decided that I no longer wanted my physical condition to be classified as a "birth injury." We made an appointment to be examined at the United Cerebral Palsy foundation of New Orleans. My mother went with me.

While I was waiting for my turn to be examined, a youngster sitting beside me was called in. When he slipped off his chair and by crawling and pushing himself across the floor, made his way into the examination room, there was a great hullaballoo and excitement because this was a major achievement for him.

Finally, they announced over the intercom that the panel wanted to see Allan Oggs. They had before them my medical records from the time of my birth through the first seven years or so of my life. When I walked into the examination room one of the physicians spoke up rather haughtily, "Excuse me, but we called for an Allan Oggs." I said, "I'm sorry, but what you see is what you've got. I'm Allan."

They were absolutely amazed. One doctor said, "He's talking." Another said, "He's walking." Finally the head of the panel asked me to walk over and shake his hand. I shook his hand and then he asked me to squeeze it. I did the best I could, which was more than he wanted.

After several hours of consultation, he looked at my mom and said, "Mrs. Oggs, if your son had been under our care for all these years and we could have taught him to feed himself, we would have been very satisfied. You don't need to worry about this boy. Someone bigger and better than we has taken care of him."

I spoke up real quick and asked, "Dr. Schlesinger, would you allow me to print this testimony about the grace of God in my life and use your name?"

He said, "By all means."

Next he asked me if I would submit to a whole battery of tests to see if they could find something in me that would help others. After many hours of testing over a lengthy period of time, they conceded that they couldn't locate anything physically or emotionally that would have accounted for my recovery. Then they asked if I would spend some time at the Center, attending PTA meetings and outings to be an inspiration to both youngsters and their parents.

"Perhaps they'll see enough in you to be encouraged to continue their pursuit of something good for themselves and their children," they said.

I did that for awhile.

Though the Lord performed a beautiful miracle in my life, he, in his wisdom, left me with a whisper of a handicap that was supposed to be very boisterous. I have never questioned his judgment.

That trip to the C.P. clinic greatly confirmed my healing to me. Before, I knew I was supposed to be doing well, but it was my mama and daddy or my relatives who told me that. They were mine and they loved me. Of course, they only saw the best. But these clinic doctors didn't even know who I was. For awhile after that, I thought about becoming a doctor and specializing in C.P.

In my sophomore year I began to feel the call of the Lord upon my life to become a preacher. When I began to let my feelings be known, people seemed to come out of the woodwork to explain to me why my physical limitations would disqualify me from the ministry. I realized that my physical condition would create some difficulties for me in the ministry, but I had dealt with difficulties all my life. Besides, there was another consideration which made the ministry seem like the best option for me. Although I was still interested in a career in medicine, I knew there was no way I could afford to attend a secular college and medical school. Bible college was a lot less expensive. With this in mind I began to seriously direct my thinking toward preaching.

It was at this time that I met Mr. Landry in the principal's office at KHS. Landry was from the state rehabilitation office. After several meetings and much testing, he informed me that I was eligible for full financial aid. The state would underwrite all my expenses at any college I chose because I was crippled.

"Son, everything we have to offer, you can have," Landry said. "You just name wherever you want to go and we'll foot the bill. Room, board, tuition—you just tell us what you want and where you want to go."

That changed the picture considerably. If money was no problem, I wasn't sure I wanted to be a preacher. Being a doctor would be a lot more glamorous—and a lot more profitable.

After much pressure from Landry to make a decision, I decided that I would fleece the Lord for his will for my life. It was, at the least, a mischievous fleece. I said, "If you want me to preach, have them call on me to be the guest speaker at the next sectional youth rally; and if they call on me to preach, make me a 'Billy Sunday' for that evening." This seemed to me an absolute impossibility. I had not witnessed for the Lord publicly a dozen words in my life that made sense.

Of course, I was invited to preach the youth rally. And I went deliberately "prepared to be unprepared." Many times since I have preached my share of "forgettable" sermons, but on this occasion, I tried to "outline a flop." I walked to the pulpit that night and the auditorium was packed wall-to-wall. Frightened and confused, I opened my Bible and read Matthew 5:16 and said, "I'd like to talk to you tonight on the subject, 'Let your light shine before men.'"

That was all I had written in my outline. I was prepared to say nothing. But after reading the scripture and announcing my title, I felt the warm hand of God touch the crown of my head and massage me to my toes. I felt an unction, an anointing—the very presence of God. And I spoke for almost an hour. At the conclusion of the message, friends were surprised and loved ones were stirred to tears. And no one was more surprised than I.

My parents wanted to hug me, friends gathered around to congratulate me, but I broke away from them all and went to the Sunday school classroom where I taught. I went inside, closed and locked the door. Then I knelt in the dark and prayed a prayer that I have lived by ever since. I said, "Lord, there's so much about you that I don't understand, but if you will allow me to occasionally feel and experience what I did tonight in the pulpit, I will preach for you the rest of my life." He has, and I have, and I have never regretted it.

After my preaching success, I went back to tell Landry I had made a decision.

"I want to go to P.B.I. (Pentecostal Bible Institute)," I said.

"You want to go to P.B. who?" he said.

Thinking real quick, because I was afraid I'd lose the scholarship, I bluffed, "You mean to tell me you are an educator, up to your chin in the system and you never heard of P.B.I.?"

"O yes," he said, "P.B.I. Well, what do you want to major in?"

I said, "Mr. Landry, I want to be a preacher."

Landry slapped his forehead and said, "O no, I didn't hear you. No way could you be a preacher. Of all the things that you could do and do well, why would you want to be a preacher? Why would anyone want to be a preacher, and most of all, why would you? You could not do it. Choose something you can do. Now what do you want to do?"

"I want to be a preacher."

After we went back and forth like this for a few minutes, he went into his office. But he forgot to close the door all the way and I heard him say, "Believe it or not, we are about to educate a Pentecostal preacher. The guy just will not go any other way."

To add even more confusion to the situation, at final exam time, I found myself thrust into an emotional battle between myself and the chemistry teacher, Mr. Carl Lazaronne.

I had flunked chemistry the year before. In the first day of the new semester, upon seeing my name on the makeshift enrollment sheet, Mr. Lazaronne had me stand, and he said to me, "Are you back again?" I'm standing there feeling like a three-dollar bill and he adds, "I'm going to flunk you again!" When he said that, I spoke back, equally aggressively, "Just try . . . try!"

I had to pass chemistry to graduate, so when final exam time arrived, I was in a panic. Now, behind my back, Mr. Lazaronne contacted my dad and told him that my grades were very good and I could flunk the exam and still graduate. (Of course, if I didn't graduate, I would forfeit my scholarship, so the pressure was really building.) Mr. Lazaronne told my dad, "I'm going to tell Allan that either he passes this exam or he doesn't graduate. I want to show him what he can do when he really 'wants to.'" My dad agreed to go along with the strategy.

So there I was at exam time, long before air conditioners crowded out windows in our public schools. I had to put separate papers under my arms to catch the sweat that dripped off my elbows. Mrs. Largesse, my history teacher, and Mrs. Danton, my biology teacher, were both pacing up and down the hall, worrying about me passing. They didn't know either that my grade was secure. So, I passed. In fact, I made an A on the exam.

Afterward, Mr. Lazaronne smiled and said, "Son, you could have flunked this exam and still passed with a C average. I just wanted to show you what you could do if you really tried." With a great deal of hostility I said, "Thanks." Then a nervous wreck went out into the hallway and told those wonderful teachers, "Thanks for your contributions."

I graduated from high school shortly after that. Graduation was a beautiful ceremony and my dad was unanimously chosen to pray the benediction. I watched big, tall fellows who hardly spoke eight words in a line without profanity stand there and weep as my dad prayed. One 6'4" fellow told me, "I've never heard anybody pray like your dad prayed." My dad was praying after investing nineteen years in a son who was now about to spring into his own future.

Allan and Gwenelda,
college freshmen

6

P.B.I.

AT P.B.I. I WAS TOTALLY on my own for the first time. Although my parents had never coddled me, I had always had plenty of family around to lend me support. Now, I was alone—except for John Cupit. He was my roommate, my shield and my constant companion in those opening weeks of my college career.

Living in the dorm with other young men presented several new challenges for me. Shaving in a public shower room was almost an impossibility. Cupit would bring me a basin of water and I'd shave in my room. I thought no one knew, but I learned later that everyone knew! Some of the guys on my floor were amazed that I could shave at all with my poor coordination. They held their breaths every day hoping I wouldn't cut my throat. I had to have someone tie my tie and button the top button of my dress shirts. I always turned back my sleeves because I couldn't button a cuff.

Academically, college was much more difficult than high school. I had to devote more time to studying. My handwriting still resembled Chinese. (Although, I will admit that when I didn't know the answer on an exam, I would make certain no one could read my writing, then plead for the benefit of the doubt. It often worked.)

However, during my first year I began to realize that, with the help of the Lord, I could be a good preacher. It became obvious that, if I were willing to pay the price, for once in my life, I could not "just compete," I could be a winner.

During my second year, I presented what was to become known as "The Speech." We had to give a speech to our speech class. I chose the category of stimulating emotion. The title of my speech was "Declaration of Independence, P.B.I." I closed with the question, "What will it be? A sword in your hand, or a ring in your nose?"

The instructor, Professor Shannon, made the mistake, in my opinion, of trying to refute some of my many negative charges. Then my second year roommate, Raymond McMorris, decided to take on Professor Shannon's rebuttal. Finally, in frustration, Shannon said, "I can't believe that 95 percent of this student body is unhappy." Raymond, who had a serious stuttering problem, leaped to his feet and said, "You, Youuuuu are right, it'sss, it'ssss 100 percent!"

Professor Shannon almost kicked me out of school. The board of my home district in Louisiana was contacted and told that I was initiating some kind of insurrection. I just sat back and smiled and reminded the professor, "If this hasn't stimulated emotions, I don't know what has." Twenty-seven years later, Melandy Shannon brought to Jackson College of Ministries the outline of the speech that I had turned in for a grade. She had borrowed it from her dad.

The highlight of my second year began the first day of school, during a prayer service. The students were in charge of this service and they needed a piano player. They started asking different ones whom they knew could play. But everyone who was asked refused on the ground that they would prefer their brother who, of course, was much better and had superior talent. So the whole service was waiting. No one knew the freshman from Antigo, Wisconsin, sitting alone. No one knew Gwenelda Vanderhoff could play. She just sat there until she couldn't take it anymore. She was scared to death, and real shy, but all of a sudden she got up, walked to the piano and started playing. I was impressed. I thought, *Here's somebody who has guts and understands the work of God.*

A few weeks later we shared a meal at General Conference, in Memphis, Tennessee. I think I may have held her hand. I didn't kiss her. There was nothing romantic between us, because I was going steady with Shirley, a girl back home. From General Conference to Christmas, Gwenelda Vanderhoff and I just barely spoke. At Christmas I took her to the railroad station to catch her train home. On a whim, I gave her a penny, but there was still nothing between us, or so I thought. She went back to Wisconsin, I went home and became officially engaged.

I thought I was very much in love with Shirley. I gave her a hope chest, and came back to school wearing her ring on my little finger. We wrote every day.

Gwenelda and I were just friends. I'd speak to her if I saw her in class or passed her on campus, but that was about it. However, I began to notice her more often and I frequently found myself thinking about her. That bothered me, because of my engagement to Shirley. But I rationalized that it was just because I was away from home, homesick, and she was available.

One night a mixed group of us were returning to our dorms. She, along with a number of her friends, made the little right turn to the women's dorm, and I, with a bunch of fellows, hung a long left toward the men's dorm. I noticed her looking my way. We had never, except at General Conference, been together on a date—never exchanged a wink. Suddenly I threw her a kiss, and I guess she liked it because she threw one of her own back to me.

By this time we were almost ten to fifteen feet apart and I asked, "Did you mean that?"

She said, "I did."

And I said, "You'd better be careful because if you did, I'm gonna marry you."

I had no idea I was going to say that. It just popped out of my mouth. By the same token, I had no idea that she cared for me. As it turned out she had been real fond of me and had been hopeful.

Curfew was at eight P.M. In about ten minutes we had to go to our rooms, so we came together, not to embrace, but to talk. In that ten minutes we set the date, the time, the place and basically who would be in the wedding. She went to her room and I went to mine. I was excited and thrilled and happy. I told Hambone (Raymond McMorris), my roommate.

I said, "Hambone, I want you to be in my wedding."

He said, "Sure, if I'm not too old, let me know."

I said, "No, I'm getting married in thirteen weeks. I'm marrying Gwenelda." I was still in shock, and now he was too!

At the same time, Gwen was in her room, excited and elated. She said to her roommate, "Donna, I'm getting married."

Donna said, "We all hope to."

She said, "No, I'm marrying Allan."

Donna said, "You're marrying who?"

Gwen said, "Allan and I are getting married in thirteen weeks." Both dorms got to buzzing and I was still engaged to Shirley!

When I finally went to bed, I was so excited. Then, I got scared. I began thinking, "She said yes very easy. Was she teasing? Maybe this is all a big joke."

I knew now that I wanted to marry Gwenelda so I lay there and plotted in my mind what I was going to do. I hadn't even courted her yet. She didn't really know anything about me or my mannerisms. I thought to myself, *I am going to put this girl on a whirlwind courtship and I'm not going to put her down until we get married,* which was kinda tough in Bible school. I kept myself looking sharp. My laundry bill went so high my dad wanted to know what had happened.

The next morning I was really filled with anxiety. I wondered, *Now what will I do if she tells me it was all a joke?*

We shared a study hall. The women sat on one side and the men on the other. I sat where I could see her, but I was afraid to look. I sat down, put my nose in a book, and wondered, *When I catch her eye, what's going to happen?* Finally, I lowered the book and gave just one glance and I knew everything was O.K.

Once I laid that anxiety to rest, I turned my attention to other concerns. How was I going to tell Shirley and my parents about my change in plans?

Shirley had a birthday in a few days and I was supposed to call her. I wished her a happy birthday, then explained the new arrangements. It was a callous way to break the news to her, but I didn't know how else to handle it.

My folks were not so easy to deal with.

Shirley's family and mine were very close. My mom was buying gifts for Shirley and building a nice relationship. I knew they would be upset, but finally I just wrote and told them Gwenelda and I were engaged.

My dad called me about 10 P.M. one night and said, "Who is Gwenelda? Allan, I want you to come home now, right now."

I said, "Dad, I don't have a car. I'm not coming."

He said, "Why not?"

I said, "Because I don't want to be pressured. I know what I want."

He said, "You get Hambone to bring you. Tell him I'll buy the gas and give him spending money for the weekend. You're coming home!" So!

We got there about daylight. I walked into the kitchen and they started in on me. They thought I was being foolish. I was just lonely and somebody had turned my head. I stood my ground. Then finally, my mother made the mistake of saying, "What am I going to tell Shirley's family?"

When she said that, my dad said, "Who cares?" He realized then that some of the debate involved more their being able to save face than my happiness and he said, "Well, that's just too bad. We'd like to save face if we can, but that's not the issue. Furthermore, I'm not surprised. I just wanted to hear it from you and to see if I could shake you." For one of the few times in my life, he put my mom in her place.

So I went back to school and Gwenelda and I dated very joyfully for the next thirteen weeks. Of course, the school had very strict rules about dating. About all you could do was go to the dairy bar on Sunday and snack in the rec hall during the week. On one end of the campus, there was a retainer wall a couple of feet high, which everyone called "the wall." You weren't allowed to sit on the grass, but you could sit on the wall. So we sat on it and talked for hours. Everyone had to have some kind of campus job and occasionally, Gwenelda would also come talk to me at the laundry where I worked. We were very much in love.

It was against the rules for boys and girls to be together off campus. The guys were allowed to go into town on certain days and the girls on different days. A lot of guys sneaked off with their girlfriends, but I had never seen a girl away from campus.

One day Gwenelda and I decided we would meet downtown. Now, I was twenty years old but we acted more like two thirteen-year-old kids who were really doing something bad. I think we rode down to the lake, where everyone went to "watch the submarine races." We were too scared to enjoy the time together. Looking back now, I wish I had relaxed, but I was thinking, *I wonder what she thinks of me for bringing her down here?*

On the way back to school, I let her out of the car blocks away and then I went on back like I'd been out all day by myself. While she was walking back to school and I was waiting, I kept thinking, *Did I mess it up? Does she still respect me?*

At the same time, she was wondering, *When I get back, will it be all over?* She made it back in time for supper. And the good feeling was still between us.

The school rule was no weddings during the school year. So school let out at midnight, May 22, and we were married at 11 A.M., May 23, 1957.

A couple of weeks before the wedding Gwen left school and went home to get ready. Then she came back a couple of days before the wedding and that's when I met her parents. Her mother was a bossy, stubborn woman. And her dad was the kind of person who would do whatever it took to keep peace. This combination didn't affect my relationship with Gwenelda. After all those hours of talking at the wall I felt I knew her, but I was surprised when I met her parents.

My parents, Nellie and Jessie, and my Aunt Viola came up. My brother was my best man. As I waited for Gwen to walk down the aisle, some of my old fears came back. I panicked, *What if this has all been a fantastic dream—a bubble that has stretched its limit and could burst any second?* Maybe she would be gone—but she wasn't. C. D. Soper, the president of P.B.I., said, "Wilt thou?" and we said, "Yes." We have been married thirty years.

We borrowed my dad's car for our honeymoon. My aunt owned a cottage two blocks from the Gulf in Bahama Beach, Florida, so we headed down there. We were supposed to stay five days, but we only stayed three. It was hot and we had no air conditioning. We didn't have much money, and had to buy groceries and cook, so we decided to go home.

Home was my old bedroom, which now became our bedroom. That summer Gwen went to work immediately at Woolworth's. I couldn't find work. Ultimately my dad took a job in order to help me.

I was at the union hall, carpenter's local 1846, waiting for a job. A job broke and they needed a certain number of men and a foreman. I raced out and called my dad. I told him they needed a foreman. My dad called the union business agent, and although he wasn't on the list, he came down, met the agent around the corner, and got the job as foreman. Of course, every crew needs a couple of apprentices, so I got one of those jobs. I made good money for those days—almost $4 an hour.

At the end of the summer Gwenelda and I quit our jobs and went back to school. I only worked a couple of hours a day and she didn't work at all and we ate in the school cafeteria. It cost me $150 a semester for her room and board. She had lots of time on her hands, so it was probably one of our easiest years. We went home for Christmas and it was then that we experienced the miracle of life, "The December conception . . . Allan is on the way."

It really has been a good marriage. From the beginning, we built a relationship that worked across the board in every respect, and I think that is one of the reasons why today we have unusually good communication.

It is not at all unusual for us to sit in the den, either together or in opposite easy chairs and talk for hours. About what? I don't know, whatever—job, house, kids, dreams.

I think I have also benefited from Gwenelda's homelife. She gave me absolute support. It wasn't always, "If that's what you want, honey," but, after a real good debate or a real good scrap, if she was convinced that I really thought something was best, or I really wanted to do it, she never tried to stand in my way. Even if she thought it wouldn't be good, it was "let's go."

And all this was built on the seed of a kind of blind faith and trust, which began with the casting of a kiss. Before that, there was nothing between us. If she hadn't thrown my kiss back, I probably would not have married her. And I am sure there would be much less of me today!

I believe that God sovereignly intervened in this situation to prevent me from making a very big mistake. Shirley was a wonderful girl, but I don't think she would have enhanced my ministry in the way Gwenelda has. I needed someone who was as committed to the ministry as I was. Only someone like Gwenelda would have supported me during my long years of struggle to make it.

My last year of school I worked selling the Mississippi

edition of the *Birmingham News.* Essentially, I was selling a Birmingham, Alabama, newspaper in Tupelo, Mississippi. It grew into a pretty good job and I spoke and represented the paper at some civic meetings in Tupelo. At the end of the school year, the *News* offered me a pretty good position. They should have known better. I was going to be a preacher.

Graduation finally arrived. Grandma Nellie, Aunt Jess, my mom and dad, and Aunt Viola came up, then followed us back as far as Kenner. I in my cap and gown and Gwen in her maternity smock, led the unique little caravan as we struck out for our first place to preach.

Graduate, P.B.I., 1958

I did and she did, 1957

7

You Can't Tell Me No

AFTER HAVING PUSHED INTO a headwind for a good portion of my life, the wind change that began in the last half of my high school years was intoxicating. When we drove off the P.B.I. campus after graduation, the feeling I had inside me was so strong and exciting, I forgot about the five-gallon container of oil that was strapped to the tailgate of the trailer. It was used oil, but we would use it again before arriving in Port Sulphur, Louisiana, about 360 miles away.

I was on my way, married to a beautiful girl, going to be a parent in four months. Hey! Not everybody graduated, but I did—and I had a place to preach. By the time I walked, in my herky, jerky way, arms going in all directions, down the aisle to the porch of our colonial-style chapel and then into the night, I had picked up such a tailwind of confidence, ambition and faith, I could almost hear the Lord saying, "We are flying very high, and a strong tailwind is giving us a tremendous forward push. We will arrive at our intended destination earlier than planned!" In fact, in my mind's eye, at least for an instant, I had already made a few of those future landings. As it turned out it wasn't quite that easy.

My dad pastored a church in Kenner, Louisiana, and a mission work of about twenty people in Port Sulphur. We were on our way to take care of the mission until the baby was born. Beyond that I had a greater ambition to evangelize. We already had a house rented, and one of the men found a job for me as a service station attendant. It was a very small house—a bedroom, bath, kitchen, and closed-in back porch located in the landlord's backyard. You had to drive up his driveway to get to our house. Gwenelda did wonders with that little place. With a few things we found at the city dump, she managed to convert the back porch into a small office for the new pastor.

On nights we were not in church, we visited between customers at the Shell station. We listened to radio reports of a Dr. Castro who came down from his mountain stronghold to overthrow the Cuban government and we talked for hours. Looking back, I am suspicious as to why we did so much talking. Probably because it was the least expensive "evening on the town." If that's true, I am thankful. We have always talked . . . and talked . . . and talked. Only very good friends talk as much as we do.

Port Sulphur is a one-street town—just the highway—with swamp on both sides. The mosquitoes were so bad that when people came into the church we sprayed them with an insect spray. After we sprayed them, there'd be enough dead mosquitoes to sweep up in a dustpan and throw out. The children couldn't play outside. The housewives didn't have clothes dryers then, so when they hung their clothes out to dry, they'd have to wrap their legs in newspapers. Cattle in Port Sulphur have been known to suffocate from mosquitoes. It is right out in the swamp.

The oil industry did a lot of offshore drilling from Port Sulphur. There was good money down there, but it was a very transient community. Men who worked on the rigs would come in and the church would flourish. Then they'd do what was called, "stacking the rig," that is preparing to move it. You'd think the church was doing real well, then they'd come in one night and say, "Brother Oggs, we're sorry but they're stacking the rig tomorrow." Well, in a small church, to have four or five families leave at one time is bad. But it gave me a chance to preach three times a week and since it was my dad's outreach, if I had serious problems he could help. It also gave me a chance to do some "hands-on" ministry, like the first time I performed a baptism.

I was baptizing a little boy about eight years old. The baptistry was the kind that required the pastor to get in the water with the candidate. I was nervous because it was my first baptism. The boy got in the water, and it was almost up to his chin. I don't know if he was afraid of the water, or just had second thoughts about his commitment, but he started motioning to me that he'd changed his mind and wanted to get out. Now, there I was in the baptismal tank, water up to my waist, and I wasn't about to get out of there without baptizing him. So while I was saying, "I baptize you in the Name of Jesus," putting his hand up to his nose, I quickly dunked him. He was blowing bubbles in the water! The poor kid really wanted out, but he got under before he got out.

In July of that summer of '58, I was also ordained a preacher of the gospel in the United Pentecostal Church. The ordination speaker, O. F. Fauss, preached a sermon titled, "Preach the Word." I was, I did, I am. Praise the Lord.

We left Port Sulphur one day when they had a bad hurricane warning and never went back. I commuted back and forth for about three months to help them out. My son went down there recently and preached. When he got back he called me, laughed and said, "Now I know why you didn't stay too long."

We moved back in with my parents while we waited for Gwenelda to give birth, and I began looking for work. I went to work for Dobbs House caterers for a few days. They were nice but my hands weren't capable of that kind of work. They claimed they were real pleased with me, but they wanted me to be willing to transfer anywhere in the country. They knew I wouldn't. Then I was out of work with a baby on the way, so I went to Sears. The personnel manager's name was Mr. Kitchen and I had heard that he was a graduate of Bob Jones University, so I knew he had a Christian background.

He interviewed me and was very nice, but said he had nothing available. When he told me that, I said, "You can't tell me that." He looked surprised and I said, "You can't tell me no." I explained that I was a preacher. I knew that he was already working about a dozen seminary students from New Orleans Baptist Seminary part time. I said, "I've got to have this job." He said again, "I'm sorry." And I said, "Sorry don't help me. I got to have work."

He sent me to be tested to see where I would work best. After I finished my test, I knew I was mentally as sharp as anyone there, but I didn't know what would happen. The longer I waited I thought, *Man, they're probably going to give me a real good position, as sharp as I am*. They put me in the toy department stockroom!

I would receive stock and stack it. Then I would sit and read, sometimes all day. I was able to get the stock organized the way they taught me in about three weeks. It was an easy job, once I got everything straightened out. But when I first got there, the stock was a mess. People had been stealing them blind. They'd put radios in trash cans, then go to the dumpsters after work and get the stuff they'd put in the trash. Or they'd remove the tags from sweaters and jackets and wear them home. This went on every day. They carried stuff off by the truck-load.

Our son was born September 26, 1958. The same little 5′3″ doctor who explained to my dad that I did not have a chance to live, now, in the same Touro Infirmary Hospital, pronounced that the one who was not supposed to live had a son: Allan Charles Oggs, Jr.

I knew C.P. was not hereditary, but I admit, I explored every square inch of Allan's body, and was grateful that he was rosy and healthy and crying; in fact, it seemed like he cried until he was almost a teenager. My boss at Sears gave me a discount on some little stuffed animals that I brought home for him for Christmas.

Allan's arrival meant we had two families in a two-bedroom house—my mom and dad, Gwenelda and I, and now Allan. You can imagine it was crowded. But aside from that, it was a very happy time for us.

Now that Allan was born, I was eager to begin preaching again. I prayed and told the Lord I wanted to preach, but he would have to provide invitations. I said if I got one two-week meeting, I would quit my job. I got the one meeting in Denham Springs, Louisiana. I stayed at Sears through the Christmas rush, then gave notice that I would be leaving the last day of December.

When I told my boss where I'd be going and what I'd be doing, he thought I was crazy. Sears appeared to be a lot more stable and for sure anything looked better than a life of faith. He offered me a raise if I would stay, but I was determined to preach.

My last day on the job was Friday. I was supposed to preach on Sunday and they cancelled my meeting on Saturday. So on the day between the old job and the new beginning, the new beginning was cancelled. I had no job and no place to go, but I didn't panic. Probably I would have panicked more if I'd had a house note or car note, but I don't think I owed a bill. My dad got me a couple of weekend speaking engagements that paid $35 to 40, and we did that into February.

If I had been desperate, I could have gone back to Sears, I suppose. But I never even considered that. I went to Sears because I had a baby on the way. My only thought was to stay there until the baby came. I guess it seems odd, because young people today are so different. They talk a lot about "keeping their options open." I never thought about having options.

When you made a commitment, you stuck to it, whether it was school, a job, or a marriage. There were times when I wasn't happy in school and all marriages have some difficult times, but to just walk away never occurred to me.

The same thing was true about preaching. I had a lot of discouraging times in the beginning, but I never considered doing anything else. I never gave Sears another thought. I knew why I went, and I did a good job. I enjoyed arguing with all those young Baptist preachers. We had a lot of good theological discussions. They thought they were right and, of course, I knew I was, so we had fun. But not to stay.

I was very fortunate that my folks supported my desire to preach and were always willing to let us stay with them in between assignments. In all the years that we were in and out of their home, we never paid room or board. Sometimes I felt like they were a little too demanding, but I guess they felt they had a right to be, since they were helping support us.

I got my first real revival in February. My father-in-law pastored a small church in Wisconsin. He had friends there and he talked one of them into inviting me for a two-week meeting.

I had to do a lot to go to Wisconsin in February. I had never owned an overcoat in my life. My in-laws sent me money for a coat and their gas credit card, so I bought gas all the way from New Orleans to Antigo, Wisconsin, on it. When we got there it was cold. I had never seen snow, except maybe an inch or two. It was down around zero and starting to snow heavily.

We were supposed to attend the Wisconsin District Conference in Clintonville, some fifty or sixty miles away. We got there about noon, after driving all the way in a blizzard. I didn't know how much wind and snow made a blizzard, so I just kept going. It was beautiful, but we barely got to the church. When we arrived, there was no one there but the host pastor, the district superintendent, my father-in-law, and myself.

Once again, at a critical point in my life, I believe God intervened directly. They had to choose two speakers, one to speak during a pre-service gathering for the young people, and another to speak at the main service. Well, either the superintendent, Richard Davis, or the host pastor, Robert Norris, had to choose himself. Neither of them was going to do that, so they chose me for the youth service and my father-in-law for the main service.

Not three minutes after they asked me, the snow stopped. To my amazement, as soon as the snow stopped, the city street department came out with snowplows and slush trucks. They hauled the snow away. The sun came out and by youth service time there was a full house and several other young preachers who might have been asked to preach instead of me had they been there. There I was, nearly 1500 miles from home, and it was either me or nobody; then suddenly the place is filled with pastors.

As a result of my preaching that night, I got a couple of invitations. My first revival was with Brother Robert Norris, who is now a missionary field superintendent in South America. He gave me that meeting sight unseen. He had never heard me. All he knew was that I was Brother Vanderhoff's son-in-law. I preached for him for two weeks and he wrote letters to some of his friends. That whole year (from February to December) I always had two or maybe three meetings ahead.

I would preach every night Tuesdays through Sunday. Monday was my rest day. Almost everybody gave me $50 or less for a week. Heading home for Christmas I had two weeks in White Hall, Illinois. I got paid $100 a week and thought I had really hit the big time.

I learned to cope with lots of snow and Yankees. They are more reserved, but that probably helped me. Most Pentecostal preachers are very emotional and require that kind of a response. But I wasn't a particularly emotional preacher. I had to take "my act" on the road. I wanted to be successful in the South, to come home again. But Louisiana and Texas are our denomination's strongest areas, and I had a lot of competition there as a young preacher.

At that time our denomination was only about 35 years old. There just weren't enough churches big enough to hire assistants, music ministers, education directors, youth pastors, or any of the other things that a young preacher can do now to break into the ministry. Then you had to travel and preach where you could. If a church had called me to pastor when I graduated, I would have accepted, but that would have been highly unusual. Since my ambition was to minister full time, my only other choice was to evangelize. I needed not only to minister, but to be accepted, and I wanted to be accepted on a larger scale than just one church. I liked being liked, and the more congregations that were pleased with my ministry, the better I felt about myself.

I think I grossed $1700 my first year. That was in 1959 and although it wasn't a great deal of money even then, if nothing happened, you could live on it. But when you've got an old car, something always happens. There again, my parents helped us. They would buy us a tire here and there. They were very pleased that I was in the ministry. My in-laws helped, not so much because I was in the ministry, but because I married their daughter. If it hadn't been for the help of my parents and my in-laws, the money I made wouldn't have carried us very far. But to me it was almost like stealing to think that I handled $1700 and all I had to do to get it was to preach. It seemed almost fraudulent—to get paid for preaching! What more could a guy ask than to preach and get paid for it?

Home was New Orleans and we always got home for Christmas. In the eyes of many people—my folks, my peers, my parents' church friends—I wasn't coming home dragging my tail. Surviving a year on the field without having to go back to Sears was considered good. I had worked hard and God had blessed me. I felt very proud. I felt like, "Bless God, I made it a year."

It was during this first year that we went to a convention in St. Louis and when we got back from the Conference all my dates had been cancelled. But on that $1700 we were able to afford five nights in St. Louis in a hotel. Of course, we had no utility bills, food, mortgage or rent. We didn't have insurance, so our expenses were minimal.

By that time we had bought another car. We were preaching around New Orleans and our old car just went to pieces. So we got a '51 Dodge. General Motors cars had automatic transmissions, but Chrysler coupes had what they called fluid drive. You could shift if you wanted to or you could start out and drive in third. It was a heavy car. It didn't have air conditioning but it did have heat—and it was in real good shape. We kept it several years.

For the next two years, I was on a treadmill, trying to support my wife, my infant son, and another child on the way. Our small family was in church every night, my wife playing the piano and singing specials—Allan on the front row, without a parent sitting beside him. In those days it was the accepted practice for wives to sing and play the piano. I didn't discover until years later that Gwenelda disliked it—and was scared to death every time she had to sing.

When we preached at a church, we either stayed in the pastor's home, or in what they called the "evangelist's quarters," which were usually located in the basement of the church. Most of the time, the quarters consisted of one large room, in which the whole family slept. We could use the church kitchen to prepare our meals, and one of the church bathrooms, which had normally been equipped with a shower. Since she was naturally shy, it was torment for Gwenelda every time we arrived at a new location and had to get acquainted with our hosts. Staying with the pastor was especially difficult for her. At least in the quarters we had a little bit of privacy.

Over the years, we stayed in a half dozen places that were broken into while we were there. In Shreveport, Louisiana, we woke up one morning when we heard a lot of commotion. Looking out, we saw policemen everywhere. Robbers had broken in, gone up the stairs, past where we were sleeping, and ransacked the pastor's study.

In Brookhaven, Mississippi, a drainage ditch ran underneath the church and the quarters where we were staying. At night, dogs, cats and other small animals got under there. They made such strange noises, I was convinced that evil spirits inhabited the place and the whole church was going to the devil.

The most frightening experience we ever had occurred in Albion, Michigan. A Yankee basement has a little half window above the ground and two thirds of the room is underground. The bathroom was out the door to the right, and the kitchen was out the door to the left. In the wee hours of the morning, Gwen woke me up and said, "Do you hear what I hear?" I said, "Oh, go back to sleep." Then I heard it. Somebody was walking upstairs! We laid there awhile and listened while they walked downstairs. We were scared to death. Allan woke up and whimpered and Gwen quickly muzzled him. Then we heard the prowler walking through the basement—for all we knew—right toward our bed.

I rolled out of bed and found a giant-sized bottle. I crept over to the door and stood there, poised to brain anybody who opened the door. I stayed at the door with my weapon until daylight—absolutely terrified.

The next morning I went to the pastor's house and said, "Man, somebody was in the church last night." He smiled and said, "It was me. I got home real late and noticed the light was on in the bell tower. I came over to turn it off." It was a good thing he didn't open that door. I would have convinced him that "things go better with Coke!"

Our life on the road was a constant hustle. We were busy every day and I still required someone to button my shirt collar and tie my tie. Gwen soon took care of that. One night while she was up to her elbows in work, getting herself and the baby ready for church, I called for her to come button my collar. "What's the matter with you?" she shot back. "Are you crippled?" "Forget it," I said. It's a little tricky, but I've been buttoning my collar and tying my tie ever since.

We attended a lot of old-fashioned camp meetings, because they were gathering places for pastors. There would always be about two dozen young preachers trying to line up preaching engagements. I would approach pastors and ask them, "Would you use me for two or three weeks?" and occasionally one would say yes. Then, the longer I talked to him, I could see a big question mark forming on his face. I could tell he was wondering if I could be understood. At times before I could get away, the pastor would change his mind, and give me some excuse like "Oh, I forgot Christmas is in December this year." Before I could sign him up and get away I would lose him.

I got to the point that I would say ahead of time, "I promise you I won't hurt you, and if things don't work out, I can move on." I tried to put him in the position where he would have to be careful not to hurt my feelings, or look like he was turning me down because of my handicap.

Many of my peers didn't do that. They came from the school of thought that said, "If it's God's will for you to preach, you will get invitations. You don't have to hustle, just make yourself available." Well, there weren't enough meetings coming to me, so I went to them. I wasn't obnoxious, but I asked. I approached pastors with the attitude, "I'm young, and we both know you could do better, but I have to start somewhere and I'd appreciate it if you could use me."

If I preached for a man and he said he enjoyed it, I always asked if he could recommend me to someone else. I kept one or two meetings ahead that way.

As an evangelist I faced two challenges. One was the same challenge that faced every other young preacher—trying to get enough meetings to continue evangelizing. I had to cope with that, plus adjusting everything in my life to my handicap.

My biggest problems in the pulpit are my articulation and my right arm. I talk slowly, and sometimes my articulation is still not as crisp or as clear as I would like it to be. I can tell if people are listening with effort. I can see their eyes dilate if they are struggling to understand me.

Sometimes a hearer will be trying so hard to understand that he will mouth the words with me. I can see people lean over discreetly and ask the person next to them what I said. Sometimes I'll repeat things three times because I can tell that they have missed it.

Someone told me once that my speech problem is an asset because it forces the audience to pay close attention. They either have to listen carefully or they've wasted an evening.

I can sense when I am headed toward a word that I can't pronounce. I can feel it coming, and I automatically adjust and use a different word. Sometimes my mind will go quicker than my mouth and I'll bite my cheek or tongue. Some pages of my Bible are speckled with blood. I've often joked that when I preach, I sweat blood. But I'm aware that I have to be careful I don't let it show in the pulpit. I get out my handkerchief and dab my lips with it. All the while, I'm wondering, *Did they catch that?*

My right arm is a constant challenge also. When I am standing, I have trouble knowing where to put it. Usually I'll start by putting it behind my back and holding it down with my left hand. Sometimes it will be stiff so long it will start to hurt. If I get relaxed, I can put it in front of me, but I can never let it just hang loose by my side.

When I am preaching, I am always thinking two thoughts. First, I am thinking about what I'm saying, trying to make sense. Second, I am thinking about signalling my arm what I want it to do, what I hope it will do, and I hope it won't do. I am constantly aware of my arm. It doesn't ever jump out without me being aware of it and wanting to do something with it.

I would love to be able to give people a good, firm handshake. Many times people like to hold onto your hand a few seconds while they talk, and I can see their faces when my hand starts to shake. Their expression says, "Oh, I didn't mean to hurt you." Well, they didn't hurt me, but it can be embarrassing.

Once when I was preaching in Brookhaven, Mississippi, the pastor leaned over right before introducing me to speak, put his fatherly hand on my knee, and said, "Brother Oggs, I don't understand it, my folks just don't like your preaching."

Another time when I was preaching in a small town in Louisiana, the pastor and his wife waged a small contest to raise a good offering. The first night the pastor received the offering for me. The second night, the pastor's wife was to see if she could raise more money for the evangelist's wife. She started off by pointing at me, "Would you look at that?" All of my spasticity and tightness showed vividly at that moment. She said, "We owe this good woman, this courageous woman, a fine offering, because when she married him she had no idea where her next piece of bread was coming from." That night I wondered why anyone would want to preach so bad that they would endure such humiliation.

With all the negatives, I still loved evangelizing. I thrilled at going night after night and being a blessing, and being appreciated. Being under the anointing of the Lord is thrilling. Having words, some of them you didn't plan to speak, come forth and meet a specific need of someone in the congregation whom you've never even met, is an indescribable high. No amount of humiliation would ever be able to offset that. And not every experience was negative.

I was preaching in a suburb of Chicago at a little mission church that met in a Y.M.C.A. clubhouse. About halfway through the song service, a one-armed drunk staggered in and fell down. It was obvious that he was a potential problem, but he just sat there quietly. Toward the end of the service, we had a time of prayer requests. He stood up and kind of staggered, and we all wondered, what next? Now, since this was a Y.M.C.A., a women's weight reduction class met after our services, and the women would often slip in a little early to weigh in on some scales at the back of the room. So, on this night the women came in as usual and here was this drunk on his feet, slurring out his words.

His name was Delbert and he said, "I want you to pray for me. I am a drunken backslider." When he said that, the power of God moved in on that little clubhouse. You could feel the compassion of people reaching out to him. Before he sat down, he knelt at the front and God really got hold of him. He prayed himself sober and began to speak in tongues.

When he got through he looked at me and asked, "Preacher, have you a flashlight?" I said, "Yeh, but it's in my car, why?" He said, "Let's go get it." I thought, *Well, why not?* We went to my car and got the flashlight. Then we went over to his car, an old Studebaker. Its body style was such that you couldn't tell if it was coming or going. I shone the light on his trunk, and it was filled with cans of beer. Delbert stood there with his one arm and I held the light while he popped all those beer cans and poured them out. There was enough beer that it formed a little rivulet and ran down into a culvert.

Several years later I came back to the area to preach and somebody stood to testify. He had on a suit and tie, his hair was combed, he was well groomed and he had an attractive wife sitting beside him. He said, "I don't know if you remember me, but I'm Delbert." One experience like that compensated for the hard times.

I have sat on the platform and been so tired or so sick, I've thought, *O God, I don't know how I'm going to get through this.* But when I got up to speak, on my first sentence, I'd feel the presence of the Lord. I would hear a certain tone in my ear and suddenly my fatigue would leave. While I was preaching I would think, *Hey, I'm healed!* Then when I sat down I'd be just as tired as before.

Sometimes I think my ministry matured because I never had anything else to fall back on. It was either preach or go back to Sears for a buck an hour. I felt like, "I have to make it here, because I have no place else to go back to." I wanted to make it preaching, and there wasn't any price I wouldn't pay.

8

Ups and Downs

I WAS PREACHING IN A PLACE called Wewahitchka, Florida, when Albert Abbey, a man with a glass eye and Army surplus clothes, walked into my life and changed it forever. (Saul, the apostle, survived with the help of Barnabas; John Mark was rejuvenated under the ministry of Simon Peter; God gave me Albert Abbey of Flint, Michigan, pastor of the great South Flint Tabernacle.)

Abbey wanted to know what I was doing preaching in a little place like Wewahitchka. I wondered what he was doing looking the way he looked asking me that sort of question. He said he was a pastor from Michigan and wanted me to come preach for him. I thought he must be crazy. I'd starve to death between Florida and Michigan. Then someone told me, "That's Brother Abbey. He has one of the biggest churches in the Midwest." He was in Florida on a fishing vacation. So I went back to him and said, "If you don't mind, I'd like to come, but I'd have to come for at least six months."

While I was preaching in Florida, I dared not get too far

away from the phone for I was waiting to hear the news of the pending birth of our second child. Gwenelda was staying at home with my folks in Kenner, and I was preaching eight to ten hours away, hoping my calculations would put me home in time for the new arrival. I arrived home in time to work three weeks for Albert P. Moss Construction Company while waiting for Debra's birth. I found more muscles on the front end of a shovel than I ever thought possible.

Almost as soon as Debra was born, we headed for Michigan where Brother Abbey had arranged my itinerary. Debra's first revival on the road came on her second week's birthday, in Baton Rouge, for Calvin Rigdon. When we left Baton Rouge on the way to Flint, we stopped by the doctor and he told us that Debra had pneumonia. We were very careful with her, but we enjoyed the whole trip. I had six months of meetings lined up!

We arrived in Jackson, Michigan, in time to attend the Michigan District Conference. The first news I heard was "Brother Abbey is in Florida fishing." My heart sank until I looked on the platform and saw men I did not know with their heads together, eyeing me up and down. After the service that afternoon, these men, acting on the recommendation of Brother Abbey, stood in line to meet me and to hear when I could be with them in their assemblies. The two years we stayed in Michigan began a financial miracle. For the first time, I could support my family and buy an almost new Buick.

Brother Abbey took good care of me. One night I preached for him and he took an offering for us to buy a new motor for our old car. There was a man in the congregation who was retired from the Buick business. He bought a car every year at the dealer's cost and he said to me, "I'm going to buy a car and at the end of the year, it will have less than 10,000 miles on it. At that time I'll sell it to you for my cost. You pick it out, the kind you want, the color you want, and in eleven months I'll sell it to you." We picked out a beautiful Buick LeSabre, hardtop sports coupe. We saved for eleven months so we would have enough money to put down on it. We loved it. The first time it snowed I ran out and tried to keep the snow off the car. Being a Southerner, I thought it might scratch the car.

I was always scheduled to preach at Abbey's church on my birthday. I would preach, then go downstairs for the annual "surprise party," and he would clothe me and the entire family.

Abbey wrote very poorly, but he could preach or teach for hours and keep you spellbound. He had a powerful congregation of mostly young couples and college students. I learned years later that he wanted me to have his church. I wish I had known. He always had a whole entourage of young preachers hanging around him, and he had a way of making them all think they were the heir apparent. I wasn't going to just get a job and hang around and wait for him to die.

I have noticed over the years that in every young ministry, if a fellow really has a want-to, somewhere in his first two or three years a surprise will surface. Someone will come along and give him a break. But it's always after they see his enthusiasm and commitment. I've had the pleasure more than once of helping an ambitious young preacher.

One night while I was preaching in Milwaukee, Wisconsin, I received an offer to pastor a church in Beloit, and I accepted. Allan Jr. was starting school in the fall, and I knew our family needed to settle down. This was my first experience pastoring. It was a small church that met in a storefront. An established church that had had problems, it had split, and the district officials had asked me, a very young man, to pastor the small group.

When I got there, we didn't have pews, songbooks, a piano or Sunday school rooms. The only thing I had inherited was a full church board. I was twenty-eight and had been on the field evangelizing for about six years. I really wanted to continue giving all my time to preaching, praying, and knocking on doors. I was so excited just to be able to be full time in the work of God.

The men of the congregation got together and arranged to pay me $75 a week, and that was all they could do. I said,

"Thank you. I'll have to sacrifice to do it, but I'm going to try to live on that." And I didn't have any better sense. I was just having fun. I was preaching, studying, praying and fasting, and knocking on doors way up there in that northern state, baptizing folks in the cold Fox River. I was in my element. Three new sermons a week and a place to preach them—what more could I ask for?

I learned many lessons in Beloit, but one of them came as a result of an extremely embarrassing experience. We attended a youth rally one Friday night. I walked through the door into the foyer and over the hum of the gathering crowd, I heard the pastor fog-horn my name. I mean he blasted it! He didn't say, "Brother." He didn't even use my last name. Just, "Allan, I want to see you in my office."

I thought, *This guy's not my superintendent, he's not my daddy.* So I decided I'd just kinda meander over to the door, but that didn't please him. He came back a second time, loud and clear, "*Now!*" Every head turned. They almost had a whiplash. I mean I hit that door as quick as I could—I didn't want to be called out again.

I got inside and he walked in behind me, slammed the door, and sat in his big old chair. He didn't offer me a place to sit. He leaned forward, looked at me and said, "You make me sick!" I said, "Huh?" And he said, "I have never been more disappointed in a young man in my life than I am in you. You turned out to be the biggest bunch of nothing I've ever been exposed to. You ought to be ashamed of yourself. You're a lazy flop."

He started on the east side of me, went to the west, to the north pole, then the south. He worked me over. He plowed me in every direction you could think of and kept on digging. He said, "Your poor family, you don't even love your wife." That was getting kind of close to home. He said, "If you loved her, you'd take better care of her. She's got two dresses, right?"

You talk about embarrassed, I didn't know how many dresses she had. I hem-hawed around and said, "Brother, I hate to tell you, I don't know how many she has—and I don't know what she has on tonight. It seems to me that you know more about her dresses than I do." He said, "I've watched and I've counted. All she has is two dresses and I'm sick of seeing her in one or the other. Your two little kids, they've got two outfits apiece and you didn't buy them. Folks in your church did. I'm just sick of seeing it. You ought to get off your sitter and get out there and take care of your family." Until then, I'd thought I was.

He said, "I built this church that you're in now and bless God, when I built this my family, my children, didn't lack for anything. You know why?"

By then I was so cowed I hardly knew where I was. I said, "No, sir, I don't know."

He said, "This is the reason why." He thrust his big hands in front of my face. "You see these?" he asked. "I do," I said. I'd either see them or eat them. He asked, "What are they?" "Hands," I said. He said, "That's right. God gave me two good hands. I took my two good hands and I gave my children everything anybody else had. I made money. I hustled. If it took me one job or two jobs or three, it didn't matter. With these two good hands I took care of my family. My wife had a wardrobe second to none; my kids had sleds and skates and toboggans and balls and bats and bicycles . . ." and he just kept on going.

I got smaller and smaller, and I thought, *If you don't back off, when I leave you won't even know I've gone. I won't have to open the door, I'll walk out underneath it.*

He kept on coming . . . "You're lazy, you're lazy. Buy your kids some nice things." I said, "All right, all right." And I tried to back the guy off. I was backing to the door telling him, "I promise I'm going to do better." I wanted some approval so bad. I was hoping he'd put a little salve on my wounds, but he left them opened. His last words were a loud, "We'll see!"

I was in tears, humiliated, hurt. Through the glass panel in the sanctuary door, I motioned to my wife to come out of the foyer. As she came out she asked, "What has happened to you?" I said, "Don't say a word. I just called you out to tell you one thing." "What is it? What's happened?" I said, "I want to tell you that I love you. With all my heart, I love you."

She said, "What! You mean you called me out of church into this public foyer to tell me that you love me?" I said, "I'm serious. I know what I've been. I've not been good to you. Look at that dress!" Not a smart thing to say. She said, "What's wrong with this dress?" I thought, *O boy. Until you can buy another one, you'd better like this one.* I said, "Well, really, baby, you do a lot for that dress, you really do." But I went on, "I want you to know *I really love you.*" She got so embarrassed, she said, "Honey, I know you love me." And I said, "O no, you don't. I've neglected you and . . ." She said, "Can I go back inside before they all think we're crazy?"

After church, I carried my two kids to the car and I did my best to wake them up. I shook them and I finally got Allan about 85 percent awake. I said, "Allan!" He said, "Yeah, Dad?" "How does a new bike sound?" He said, "Sounds good." I mean my heart was big and I was trying to make restitution. I said, "Wake up, boy, I'm fixin' to buy you the whole store. Anything you . . . are you awake?" He was sound asleep again.

I took them home and lined them all up—Gwen, Allan and Debra—in the living room. I said, "Please, even if you are sleepy, please help me. Hear me out. Stay awake long enough to let me tell you what I'm going to buy for you. I love you, I'm gonna buy you . . ." The whole time I was talking they were leaning toward the bedroom, and the first time I slowed down they took off. And there I was on Friday night, and Saturday you can't find a job.

Sunday morning I walked to the pulpit and looked out and there sat the daughter and son-in-law of the man who had worked me over. I thought, *Man alive, the big dog got me Friday and the puppies are here to get me today!* I could hardly keep my mind on my sermon enough to preach, but I got through it somehow.

After the service my wife and I hung around and hung around, thinking we could "out-hang" them, but they just stayed. Finally I said, "We're going home now and eat a little bite (until then we had called it dinner). Would you like to eat with us?" They said, "Yeah, we'd like to go home with you." My heart sank.

I knew the house was clean, but we had paper drapes from Woolworth's and I knew there weren't two chairs in the dining room that matched. We didn't have china or crystal or silver. All we had were hand-me-downs or made-overs. But we went home to eat.

We sat down and I asked the woman's husband to give thanks for the food. As soon as he said, "Amen," she said, "You know what? When I was growing up I had everything." And I thought, *Yeah, and I've had enough!* I wasn't going to let her do to me in front of my children what her father had done earlier. I said, "I am aware that you had everything." I was also thinking, *I know how much, where you hung it, piled it, stored it, and played with it.*

She said, "We did. My brother and I had everything we wanted except what we wanted most." I said, "Hey, wait a minute." I didn't want to hurt her feelings, but I knew, if her daddy told the truth, she didn't have a toy box, she had a toy boxcar. I mean, she had it.

She said, "My daddy had this thing—he would get in his car and cruise the neighborhood and check the other kids' toys, and if he saw some toys that they had and we didn't, he'd have to get them. He's sell magazines door-to-door in distant cities and stay gone for days. To us kids, it seemed like he was never home. He was always out there making money, buying us junk."

When she said that, I had an instantaneous transition in my spirit. I had no hard feelings for the guy. I thought, *How sad! He's done all that to buy something, but he hasn't bought a thing. All that hustle, all that go, all that aggressiveness, all that expenditure, all that energy and what he hoped to secure, eluded him.*

She said, "We'll leave here and I'll knock on my daddy's door . . ." I thought that was strange. I never knocked on my daddy's door. She said, "I'll knock on his door and he'll open it. He'll squeeze me and kiss my cheek and when he does, something inside me will weave into a knot. I can't help it, there's something inside me that says, 'Hey, Dad, don't touch me! When I needed your kisses, where were you then?'"

Here was a good man, a good preacher, involved in a good, legitimate effort—but he "majored in a minor." What she wanted most she did not get at all. I learned a valuable lesson in that "weekend seminar." The need of this hour is for men who are not misled by materialism or fooled by peer pressure.

It was ironic that I should be blasted for being lazy because Gwen and I both worked while we were in Beloit. Gwenelda was babysitting and working at the corn curl factory. She worked at the factory all night, then got home to take care of some twelve to twenty kids during the day.

I sold Fuller brushes door to door. I needed to make a certain amount of money in a day. Some days I'd make it in a half-hour, on others it would take the whole day. Naturally, seeing what I could do in a half-hour, my supervisor wanted me to work all day every day, but I didn't want to. I'd make my money and go home. I was out making my quota one day and the lady said, "I'm glad to see you, but my children have the measles." I told her that didn't matter and I went in and made the sale.

Several days later I woke up in the night convinced I was dying. From the top of my head to the soles of my feet I was sore. I got up and prayed, "Lord, if this is it, I want to make sure that everything's right. If there's anything I need to do, just tell me." The next day, it got worse. I took a bath and went to bed. My wife walked into the room, looked at me and screamed, "You've got the measles." Until I heard it was measles, I really thought I was dying. Every muscle in my body hurt—and all to make a sale for the Fuller Brush Company.

I'm sure that my handicap helped me some. I'm a pretty good salesman, but when you knock on a door at zero degrees outside, and you can't write too well anyway and your hands are almost numb, you arouse some pity. So I did well. Fuller Brush wanted me to become a full-time salesman. They offered me trips, suits, all kinds of things. They just knew they could buy me with incentives; but they didn't have any more success than Sears. I didn't want to do anything but preach.

We stayed only two years in Beloit. It was a very difficult place. The church was full of criss-crossing factions and divisions. In the 22 months I was there I went down to 144 pounds. My wife was the smallest she had ever been. When I resigned no one called me to another church so I just went back on the field evangelizing.

When we started traveling again, we decided to send Allan to live with my folks. He had started school when we were in Beloit and he'd had some problems. We felt he needed a more stable environment. It was the first time we had been separated from either of our children and it was hard on all of us. It was made more difficult by the fact that our finances were really tight. I was preaching in Indiana and money was so short that we couldn't visit Allan very often. He was down in Louisiana for months at a time without us seeing him.

While we were on the road, my dad had a couple of heart attacks. I received word that the few people he had left in his church were restless. He asked if I would come home and be his co-pastor. My dad had been good to me and it looked bad, so I went back to Kenner. That would prove to be a major mistake, but at the time I felt I had no choice.

Evangelizing, preaching and singing every night, 1959

Port Sulphur, Louisiana—our first mission assignment, 1958

9

Detour in Kenner

WHEN WE ARRIVED IN KENNER, the church was barely holding its own. After his heart attacks, it simply became too difficult for my dad to handle the church by himself. So, in the fall of 1966, I became co-pastor of the First Pentecostal Church of Kenner. My dad could only afford to pay me $100 a month. My rent alone was $125.

I was back home where my ministry began, in another small church that required both Gwenelda and me to work secular jobs. Gwenelda found a pretty good job with a bakery chain. I had a succession of jobs. My best one, I suppose, was throwing 335 *Times-Picayune* morning papers from the window of my little VW. I got to be pretty good at steering the car with my knees while rolling and binding the papers with a rubber band and throwing to my left out the window and to my right out and over the top of the car.

I also picked up some odd jobs of painting and laying asphalt tile floors. I had never done either before, but why not? Grant you, I wasn't graceful, but I could do a good job. I painted four bakeries for the chain Gwenelda worked for, two-tone paint jobs at that, and some of them by street light or car headlights after church. The only problem occurred the night I parked the car too close to the building and splattered paint all over it. It looked like it had the white measles.

After I had been home about six months, the church was starting to grow and my dad began a building program. Deep down he had a love for God and wanted to do something for God, but to him, doing something for God had a lot to do with building. Sermonizing or building a relationship with people was not his thing. Therefore his teaching, preaching, and pastoral abilities were limited. My mother did most of the counseling on the phone. He felt most fulfilled when he could move a wall, or do something with his hands. He was a super craftsman.

We had a running battle over the length of the Sunday morning service. Since my dad didn't particularly like to preach, I preached on Sunday, mornings and evenings, and he taught on Wednesday nights. He was such a layman at heart, he always let church out before twelve on Sunday so the congregation could beat the other churches to the cafeterias. I had been preaching up north, where Sunday services were often powerful and could sometimes go until one or two in the afternoon. So, when I came home, I told him we were going to hold services until noon.

He played all kinds of games to try to get me to quit early. He'd sing or make announcements, anything he could to delay the service so I couldn't start preaching until a quarter of twelve. When that didn't work, he tried the opposite approach, giving me the pulpit at 11 A.M. "What will you do if I give you too much time?" he asked. I said, "I'll whistle." The church was only a block away from the fire station and it blew a noon whistle, but only on Sundays. So I told him we would not let church out until we heard the noon whistle. Dad tried every scheme he could think of to throw me off.

My dad was a very demanding man and he made a lot of demands of both Gwenelda and me while we were in Kenner. I think he was harder on Gwenelda than he was on me, or maybe I was just used to it. I think he saw I had a ministry developing and he did not want anything to interfere with that. Gwenelda was going to dress right, she was going to be superactive. She wasn't going to miss anything. She was going to work harder than any other woman in the church with no slack at all. He didn't dislike her. He just knew that I couldn't survive a bad marriage. Few of our pastors divorce, remarry, and keep on preaching. His bossiness with Gwen was his way of training her (although she didn't need it) to be a suitable wife for me.

During the six years that we traveled, our only permanent place was his home. I lived at home until I got married and then I lived at home after I got married, so I wasn't aware that he controlled me, or dominated me, but maybe he did. I was aware of wanting his approval for my ministry and never getting it. He told other people how proud he was of me, but he never told me. If I made a mistake, though, I heard about it. Then he would just eat me up. "That was a sad excuse for a sermon. Dear God, you must have spent five minutes on that." If I preached well and the church was blessed, he never said a word. If I did bad, sometimes before I left the platform he'd let me know it smelled. He never approved any innovations I wanted to try, but if they worked, of course they were his idea. Even when the church began to grow again, he never thanked me or gave me a single compliment.

It wasn't just my dad's approval that I needed. I wanted everybody's. My handicap had been a liability in everything I have ever done, except the ministry. There it became an asset because it was an attention-getter and people admired my effort in overcoming it. I think that encouraged me to pursue the way I did. I suppose I thought at first my motivation was entirely spiritual—I just loved Jesus! But perhaps it wasn't, I realize now. The approval and the recognition were very important to me.

After so many years of having to stand by and listen while your friends fought over who had to take you on a ball team, it was gratifying to go to a camp meeting and leave with ten invitations while the other preachers my age had four. A very few in my whole class at P.B.I. have enjoyed the experiences I've had.

I had friends who didn't make it tell me bitterly, "You cripples get all the breaks." For years I resented that. One man who gave up preaching to sell cars accused me of using my handicap. I said, "Let me tell you about the breaks I got. While you were working for a steady check, my wife and I were getting the breaks in a Dodge, with a kid and then two kids, a diaper pail, diapers, a collapsible baby bed, a suit and a dress apiece. We moved every thirteen nights. And while we were getting our breaks, you were taking home a regular check every week. While you chose that, I chose to go the easy way." He didn't say anything after that. The sad thing is that he could preach right now. He has a tremendous mind, personality, charm and nice looks. He may have used only half his mind, but that regular income meant everything to him. He gave up the ministry for that . . . a check every week for twenty years.

I tell my classes and I told my son, "Your success will be in direct proportion to your sacrifice. Not just in the ministry, but in anything in life. You will be as good as you are willing to hurt." My ego need wasn't just to say, "I'm good," but to say, "I'm as good as you and I'm handicapped."

If I didn't get the approval I needed from my dad, I was beginning to get it from other places. As soon as he got strong enough, I began preaching here and there around the country. Although I considered myself an evangelist, I was not the stereotyped evangelist who could come into a church and reap a big harvest of new converts. Actually, such preachers are revivalists. They are usually real dynamos, superemotional types. I didn't carry chairs to build my illustrations. I stood behind the pulpit and painted my illustrations with words. My peers might go to a place and twenty people would receive the

Holy Ghost. I'd go right behind them and three would get it, because I had a different type of ministry. That bothered me until I got some words of wisdom from one of the greatest preachers I ever heard—Brother George Glass, Sr.

I was preaching for Brother Glass in Jonesboro, Arkansas. One morning he asked me to go with him to make a house call. He picked me up in his big old Pontiac Bonneville. We drove out to the outskirts of town and turned down a rutted dirt road which led to a large cotton field. He stopped the car and turned off the engine. We sat silently for a few minutes. Then he began speaking slowly to me. Using the cotton field as a "visual aid," he showed me my place in the ministry.

He began by talking about the importance of carefully planting the cotton seed. Then he said, "When it is time to harvest, truckloads of people will come in to pick who can't even read. They can't lay out a field or plant a crop. They live in shacks, and migrate, following the crops. Their hands are quick and they are tremendous natural-born pickers—but they have no real agricultural skill. After somebody plows and plants, your job, Allan, is to weed and water and *pamper* the crop. You have to see to it that the good work which has already begun will last long enough for a skilled hand to come through and pick it. Or to keep it from spoiling after it's been picked."

I have never forgotten that story. It gave me new confidence in myself and my ministry. However, I still had to do what I could to keep invitations coming.

I experimented with a lot of different challenges. One of them was, I would go into a church and tell the pastor that I could double his Sunday school attendance in a week. If he said, "No, you can't," I knew I had half my work done right then. We would bicker playfully back and forth from the pulpit. I could always do it if I could get the congregation excited about the fun of it. I'd say, "Whoever brings the most new people to Sunday school will get a piece of candy six feet tall." Then I'd go out and get a stick six feet tall and tape peppermints to it. My success was built on successfully goading the pastor until he and his people would work harder than ever to beat me. I seldom lost and it was fun!

One of my most memorable and hilarious weekend trips was to the Gateway College of Evangelism in St. Louis, Missouri. The guest speaker who had been there a few weeks earlier had illustrated a point in his sermon by telling of a preacher he knew who had C.P. He said the man's walk was unsteady, his writing was just about illegible and wherever he went to preach, people had to feed him. He painted my picture to be a sad one. So when I walked in three weeks later, did my share of eating in the school cafeteria, and got lucky and won a couple of games of handball, it became a real fun trip. Pastor Winfred Black even offered me $10 if I would go out with him and the preacher who told the story and allow him to feed me at the table. I said, "It's a deal," but Pastor Black backed out at the last minute. I was willing to do anything for fun and ten bucks!.

While I was in Kenner, I was invited to preach for Nathaniel A. Urshan. At the time, Urshan pastored Calvary Tabernacle, the largest church in our fellowship. Today he is the General Superintendent of the U.P.C. International. It was quite an honor to be asked to preach for him. When I first arrived, he introduced me to his wife, Jean. She took one look at me and whispered, "Nathan, where did you get this one?" After the service, he turned to her at lunch and asked, in front of us all, "Jean, now what do you think of my preacher?"

My second visit to Calvary Tabernacle proved to be an unforgettable experience. I traveled with Urshan to a sectional conference in Columbus, Indiana, and between the city of Indianapolis and Columbus, Brother Urshan absolutely took me apart piece by piece.

He explained to me that I was using my handicap in a way that wasn't fair. I was thinking as a pastor that I was really capable of being stern, being tough, making people hew the line. What I didn't know was that if I weren't handicapped, those same people wouldn't take all that.

Urshan said that my rude preaching was not as well received as it appeared. "People receive it and just sit on it for fear of hurting you. You've got the people in a position where out of kindness to you, not your message or your concepts, they won't say anything. You've become a bully! You are using your handicap in a way that is building resentment toward you." He timed his lecture so that when he got through we were there.

It was the same old thing. It went back to Fritzi saying, "I won't hit you, because you're crippled." I thought I had overcome that by now. I was indignant. I felt Urshan was out of line. Who did he think he was? He hadn't known me long enough or well enough to talk to me like that. The last thing I wanted to admit was that I used my handicap.

That whole night during the service, I kept thinking about what he had said, and I didn't like it. After the meeting we went out to eat and it was a long time before we got back to the hotel. When we got back, about 1 A.M., he was ready to help me. We talked for hours as we lay in twin beds in the dark and he explained to me how I would need to be careful not ever to position somebody in such a way that they couldn't respond because of my handicap. He said my handicap was a door opener, a fantastic testimony, but I never wanted to use it in such a way that I could hit somebody then jump back and say, "Ha, ha, you can't hit me." When he got through he said good night. I went to sleep. But I felt like I had been to school again.

We ate breakfast and that was it. I preached that whole week and there would have been 2,000 other preachers who would have loved to have preached for him—or just to be in the room with him and hear him talk. He didn't use me for what I could do for his church, he did it to help me.

After that, I preached for him almost every year. Whenever I preached, I would stay in his home. His housekeeper, Olga, was from Jamaica. When I arrived at the front door Olga would take care of me like royalty, even as far as ironing my underwear. After one trip I went home and told my wife that Olga had ironed my underwear—and I wanted it ironed from now on. She said, "If you do, you can go back to Olga."

Even when I preached for Urshan, I never got a compliment from my dad. I remember coming home after my first trip to Calvary Tabernacle. I was popping my buttons. I had flown there to speak in our largest church and stayed in a hotel. That was downtown stuff for me then. He never asked how it went, how many people were there, how many got baptized, how many received the Holy Ghost, or anything. He just said, "Allan, take out the garbage." I don't know if he planned it that way or if it was accidental, but it seemed that every time I was at his house, there was always some trash for me to handle.

My dad died three years after I came home. At the time, the remodeling on the church was about 60–70 percent completed, so I took it on myself and finished it. That was my first shot at carpentry—I liked it. We stayed two years after my dad died and that proved to be a big mistake. In fact, if I had it to do over again I don't think I would have gone to Kenner at all. Not only did it stymie me and put my ministry on hold, I didn't accomplish what I went to accomplish. I went to be a superson to help out my dad in his last few years. And by the time my dad died, we had scuffled enough on issues that some of the things that brought me home were lost. When Dad died, I was still listening for sounds and reaching for crumbs of approval that never came. What I went to build, our rapport, was less than when I arrived.

In spite of the fact that Gwenelda and I both worked two and three jobs the entire time we were in Kenner, it was a financial disaster for us. We arrived with A-1 credit and a late model Buick. In five years we left with a VW and owing more than twenty creditors.

Our credit was good enough when we arrived that for three years we borrowed this to pay that and did real well. But then it all began to close in on us. By the time we left, we were in financial chaos. We had to move into the upstairs of the church. It had no windows, no ceilings or walls, just the exterior sheeting. Gwen and I took turns sitting up nights watching the kids to make sure the rats didn't get them.

When I got one note behind on my Buick, I called the GMAC representative and said, "I'd rather have you take it now while I only owe you one payment, instead of stretching it out until I owe you four notes and you'll still have to take it." Finally, we went down to the Consumer Credit Bureau. I'm not ashamed of that. In fact, I'm quite proud of the fact that I paid every dime, and, as promised, I got my A-1 credit rating back.

We did have some shocking but exciting news while we were in Kenner. Gwenelda was not, after all, wrestling with a lingering stomach virus. Hers was a condition that would pass in a few months, nine to be exact. I was so excited, I stopped traffic on a busy highway to tell a friend. Gwen was in a state of shock. In the car sobbing she told me, "And you know what, honey, right after the doctor told me I was pregnant, I looked up on the wall and there was a picture, big as day, of a huge pregnant woman with the caption, 'I should have danced all night.'" She didn't think it was very funny.

Jody was born on November 12, 1968, and she still refers to herself as "the little mistake that brought great joy to the family." No statement could be more true. Though raised and spoiled by aging parents, a doting big sister and brother, she has done amazingly well. The parents finally settled down after going to the hospital for three false alarms and the dad explaining to the floor nurses, "Any information you need concerning this delivery, you ask me, 'cause I've got all the answers." Gwen was home from the hospital and back at work at the church day-care center in less than a week. She never missed a Sunday at the piano.

With another addition to the family, it became more apparent than ever that I could not continue to pastor in Kenner. So, I grabbed my black book and started putting together a schedule. I flew to Denver to begin my new evangelistic tour with Pastor Billy Parker. I was there three days when a church in West Helena, Arkansas, called and offered me the pastorate. I didn't know it at the time, but that call would finally mark the beginning of the end of the long years of struggling.

10

Color Me Green

AFTER PAYING MY DUES for twelve years, my life and ministry shifted into a new dimension in West Helena. This was the beginning of the green years for me.

This was my first, for-sure, full-time pastorate. The only disadvantage was that we would live in a church apartment. However, this did not last long.

The two are actually twin cities, West Helena and Helena. The total population of both cities was about 20,000. It's a rural area and the population is pretty equally divided between those people who have a lot of money and those who have very little. There is not much of a middle class.

The affluent in the congregation were very kind to those who had little, but those who had little were very hostile to those who had something. The poorer members of the church always voted no on any expenditures of church money. Ironically, we brought most of them to church in a bus on Sundays. It was a "secret" joke that we sent the bus to pick up our "no" votes. When we moved into the beautiful new parsonage, one lady said to my wife, "Sister Oggs, how are you going to feel talking to and living next to a lawyer?" My wife said, "Well, I'm going to feel like I feel when I talk to you."

Attendance ran at about 125 people. After I got there I found that the pastor before me, a dear friend, Cecil Greenway, had been rather unique. The people claimed that he told them it was O.K. if they couldn't afford to pay tithes. I didn't think that kind of preacher existed! So I was elected, settled in and found that there were not many more than a half dozen people faithfully paying tithes.

Going to West Helena did not improve our finances much. It was two years before we could pay off all the bills we had accumulated in Kenner and get our credit restored. During that time I had a wreck and totaled my old VW. That put me in a real bind—I had to have another car. But under the agreement we had signed with the consumer credit bureau, I was prohibited from taking on any new debts. Finally, one of the men in the church bought a car, had it titled in his name, and I made the payments to him. West Helena was a real blessing to us, though, because it enabled our family to stay together.

We moved into the back of the church in a two-bedroom apartment, and what used to be the church kitchen. They also moved a few partitions around in the old Sunday school rooms so that we ended up with two bedrooms, a kitchen, living room, and bath.

One day not long after we arrived, Gwen and I were driving around town and we came to a nice residential neighborhood. Gwen especially admired one particularly beautiful house and she said to me, "When you come into your kingdom, that is where I want to live. That's my house." Of course I assured her it was hers, somewhere in my future kingdom.

A couple of months later, I went out of town for a few days and when I got back the church secretary, Sylvester Huling, said we had an appointment in town. I was still a little cautious with my position in the church and I questioned his making an appointment for me. But he wouldn't take no for an answer. He gathered Gwen and me up in his car and took us to her "dream house." It seems the church had heard about her dream. As we walked around inside, my wife turned to me with tears in her eyes and said, "Look, baby, it even has windows!"

When she said that it hurt me deeply. I said to the secretary, "I don't know why I'm here, but we are leaving now." I could see Gwen was becoming intoxicated with the house and I knew I couldn't afford it. The secretary was only about 5′2″ but he said, "No, you're not leaving. Dr. Traylor and the church board have investigated. If you want to live here, it's yours."

I was overwhelmed. We had only been in West Helena a short time. It usually takes a congregation that long just to decide if they like you. They're still trying to figure out how much they are going to have to adjust to get used to you and they are hoping that you will adjust in order to be liked.

We moved on a Wednesday night after church. It was like Cinderella going to the castle. We had a big old blue Sunday school bus painted like Noah's ark and we moved into that very nice neighborhood between 10–12 o'clock at night with pick-up trucks and cars and the "blue goose." The house had a fireplace, air conditioning, and a screened-in front porch. Before we moved in, they had completely redone the whole place. It even had wallpaper. We were downtown. We walked around for days unable to believe it.

While we were in Helena, Allan began having terrible problems in school. He was fourteen and flunking everything. We decided to find out if he just didn't have the brains, or if there was some other problem. So we took him to a state agency to be tested and his tests indicated his I.Q. was quite a bit above average. There was no physical reason why he was failing. The agency people asked if we would like to try to find out the problem.

By the time we went to see them, we had moved into our new house. Allan had his own room for the first time ever, but he would not, or could not, sleep in it all night. He would hunt rabbits all day, play basketball, fight—he was all-boy—but at night he had to sleep in our bed or if not in our bed, by our bed. Well, we didn't connect that with the problems he was having in school. But when we went to see if we could do something about his grades, all three of us wound up in counseling.

The first day they called Gwen and me in but not Allan. Now I'm kind of passive, if not slow, but my wife is a real fighter. She demanded to know why he wasn't in there, since he had the problem. As it turned out, it was our problems that were causing his. Gwen had some things in her childhood that had affected some of her thinking and I had some things that had twisted me. Allan's difficulties resulted from our emotional tangles.

Everything the state had—psychologists, psychiatrists, and marriage counselors—was available to us. We went once a week for an hour-long session. They would discontinue a session right at the most heated moment. Then that would give you a whole week to sort everything out. We'd leave confused and irritated, vowing to each other that this was the last time, but the next week, back we'd go for another session. It became very involved, and Allan was still sitting out in the hall.

We had been in counseling for weeks when I made a crucial breakthrough. I could sense it coming before it arrived. It was a little like hitting a home run—when you get to third, you know home is coming. I was talking ninety miles an hour and all of a sudden I could feel that sensation. I knew that I was about to get someplace where I had never been. Suddenly I said, "Hey, that's me! I'm talking about me!" For the first time it dawned on me that I was seeing myself with no secrets. I wasn't inhibited. I broke out of my shell right there into a world of colors—no longer hiding in all that cloudy, gray stuff.

Finally, they asked if we would like to talk to a marriage counselor. Gwen popped off right away, "There's nothing wrong with our marriage." I said, "I think we're doing real good, but if you can make it better, sure." So, we talked to the counselor and it was very enlightening. On our last session, the counselor sat like a cowboy, with the chair back facing us. He got right in my face, nose to nose. It was obvious he was trying to light my fuse, and he did. He pushed me until I drew my fist back. I wanted so badly to hit him, but immediately I did what I had done all my life. I lowered my fist and voice and said with a superior tone, "That's O.K., I understand." The truth was I didn't know how to fight, because no one would ever fight me.

In our home, Gwen was the fighter. I would get the "scrap pot" boiling real good. Gwen would be all red in the face and ready to fight, then I would always back off, and say loftily, "I'm going to get some coffee. When you get ahold of yourself, I'll be back and we'll discuss this calmly." Well, that can drive a person up a wall. That is worse than being hit. It's not fair. I'm still not a good fighter, but since that day I've become better.

It was such a quick lesson for me. The church had a problem which had existed for years. I went home from the doctor that day and the leader of the little "insurrection pocket" called me. She just bored holes in my head. I listened and hung up. I walked to the pulpit that night, and said, "Folks, I'm sorry I'm late, but this is why. Sister X called me and said . . ." I gave the whole problem to the church then added, "I want every man in this church that's going to back me to come up and sit behind me on the platform and if all of you don't come, I'm gone."

I had learned how to fight! Before I would have said, "Oh, there's nothing wrong," while I was getting my brains beaten out. Publicly, I'd say everything was fine, while that woman was driving me nuts. Well, they had never heard anything like that from me and it solved the problem to a large degree.

As a boy I would do my share of cussing and spitting and hitting, but who would hit a cripple? They couldn't get by with that. I would irritate people until they cussed me out, but they couldn't—or wouldn't—hit me. So they would do to me what, in later life, I would do to other people.

After that breakthrough in our counseling session, they started helping us with Allan. We moved him back one foot at a time from our bed. Then we moved him outside and locked the bedroom door. And that meant when we opened the door in the morning, he would be at the doorsill with pillow and blanket and his nose pressed to the crack at the bottom of the door as close as he could get to us. Of course, his friends didn't know that because when he woke up he'd be barefoot and tough.

I've told this story several times preaching because so few people will admit they need emotional help, help with their feelings and thoughts. I have no regrets for doing so because we needed it. I was blessed to get a doctor who didn't blame all my ills on being Pentecostal. Not one time did anyone ever allude to the fact that my being too conservative or too orthodox was my problem. So many people whom I've pastored will go to an M.D. for a scratch, but they can have their mental and emotional capacities draining out their ears—and they won't go for help. I received the Holy Ghost in 1951 and next to that, the breakthrough I experienced in counseling was the most enlightening experience I ever had.

West Helena was good for us, but while I was there I became aware of a new program being developed in the Youth Division of UPC called Youth Redemption. It was designed to minister to youth who were involved with drugs. I sat down and, with one finger of each hand, typed a resumé and shared with the President of the Youth Division, Kenneth Haney, my ideas, burdens, and ambitions for the program. I was asked to join the staff and we moved to St. Louis.

I don't think I could have taken the job in St. Louis if we hadn't come to grips with things in West Helena. I was on the road all the time. And Gwen and I had a real good discussion about it. I liked to travel but she wanted to stay home with the kids. The bottom line of our discussion was, "Why can't we be happy, with you doing what you like to do and me not resenting it, and me doing what I like to do and you not resenting it?" I don't know if we could have done that before.

My traveling had always been a problem because I wanted her to go on every trip. After our counseling sessions she felt strong enough to just say she didn't want to go and that I was being unfair to try to make her go or to try to bribe her with gifts. That was one of my favorite techniques. If I were going on a trip in June, I'd start buying her gifts in May. "Oh, this is just a little something I picked up for your trip." Well, she knew what I was doing. By the time the trip came, she'd feel like a dirty dog if she didn't go.

On those trips I would be preaching, but I also wanted us to have some fun. We were off without the kids, it could have been like another honeymoon. But honeymoons don't work when one person feels coerced into going. She would try to give me a good trip, but she really didn't want to go. Then that would cause tension because I'd think, *Man, I've got a hundred bucks in this trip*. So we don't do that anymore. She is always invited and welcome and every now and then, she'll say, "I'd like to go with you." Then we have a great time.

Also, after that I stopped asking Gwen to do a lot of things in the church unless I absolutely had to. She can play piano and organ, lead the choir, do all of that and do it well—but she doesn't necessarily enjoy it. So now I only ask her to if we have nobody else. Before she did everything because she thought the minister's wife was supposed to. I think that phrase "supposed to" is a monster. We went to Kenner because I felt I was supposed to and it was the biggest mistake of my life.

Going to St. Louis made a dramatic and instantaneous change in our finances. For the first time in all of our traveling, Mayflower Moving Company moved us. That was a treat. And unbeknownst to me, my wife packed only one suit (new) and two shirts (fairly new). She discarded the rest of my tattered and worn wardrobe, but I immediately began buying Hart Schaffner and Marx suits to replace it. We were also able to buy our first house.

Part of my new-found prosperity was that I was able to buy additional life insurance. I had an insurance physical and they almost killed me proving I was healthy. They put me through so many tests—"Just one more up-and-down, Mr.

Oggs . . ." They even had me in a corner with a jump rope. Can you imagine me, with my coordination, jumping rope?

Finally, I sat in the chair while the doctor went into his inner office. Through a crack in the door I could hear him talking to his staff. He said, "You won't believe what I have in my office." I didn't know what that meant. I thought it could go either way. I listened as he described how he thought I should not be doing what I'm doing and he painted a very dismal picture. Then he told them, "I'm going to ask him to take one more test, to walk down the hall, and I want you to sneak out and see how well he does. He's a little stiff-legged, but after he leaves I'll tell you the whole story."

I was sitting there thinking about how I had just walked twenty-two miles with Nathaniel Urshan for a missions fund drive—it was supposed to be twenty but I had made a wrong turn. I thought I would have some fun with them. He came in and said, "Reverend, there's one more test, one more activity you have to do before I can pass you. You have to walk." I jumped up and walked around my chair and said, "How's that, doc?" He said, "No, no, that won't do it. I want you to go outside and walk down the hall. Just go as far as you can walk, then walk back." I said, "Okay."

I walked down the hall about half-way, then whipped around real quick and caught his whole staff admiring the grace of God in my life. They thought they were seeing something that I had achieved over the years but actually they were just seeing the fingerprints of the grace of God all over my body! I did my best to explain this to them.

Shortly after I arrived in St. Louis, I received one of the highest honors bestowed on preachers in our denomination. I was invited to preach at the annual General Conference, which was held that year in Miami. Although I was grateful finally not to have to worry about money, I think I appreciated that recognition (going to St. Louis and being asked to speak at General Conference) even more than my improved financial status. At last, I was able to relax. Everybody in UPC knew me. They knew how I walked, how I talked. I didn't have to go anywhere and be uptight. I had reached the place in my ministry where people realized that I wasn't going to go away and they accepted me. In Miami I preached on the subject, "Today Is the Beginning." God blessed in an unusual way and that message opened many doors for my ministry. Because of the interest that message generated, Word Aflame Press published a collection of my sermons which sold several thousand copies.

Several years later I met a lady who told me that she heard a tape of the message while a patient in a mental hospital, and it changed her life. She began waking fresh each morning telling herself, "It is not over. It is only beginning. 'Today is the beginning of the rest of my life.'"

So, between April and October I experienced a lot of firsts. I was moved by Mayflower, bought my first expensive suits, my first house, was approved for extra life insurance benefits, and preached at General Conference. I was really flying high. But God has a way of humorously bringing us down to earth. The morning after I had preached at General Conference to great acclaim, my old green station wagon stalled out in the driveway of our posh Miami hotel. My peers who had applauded me the night before now watched while the doorman pushed me off. If I thought I had arrived, I was being gently reminded that I still had a long way to go!

St. Louis, when we were all younger—Jody, 4, Debra, 12, Allan, 14

11

See You in St. Louis

YOUTH REDEMPTION WAS ONLY a "paper dream" when I arrived in St. Louis. It was a concept that needed to be developed. My job as field representative was to be involved in developing it and to find funding for it.

I arrived in April. In April and May I designed brochures, built booths and put together a promotional program. In June, July and August, I hopped all over the country promoting it. I attended eighteen or nineteen camp meetings, establishing a constituency for Youth Redemption Ministries. By the end of August, Youth Redemption was a household word in our fellowship and so was my ministry. The project was off and running—and within budget.

Youth Redemption started as a youth rehabilitation effort modeled after Dave Wilkerson's Teen Challenge and I had no trouble getting support for it. I presented a solution to an obvious need and people responded enthusiastically.

My promotion was 85 percent preaching. Every other department had flow charts, flip charts and slide shows (side shows). I had no material but a brochure and a pledge card. That caught everybody off guard. The Lord gave me one sermon which I preached five nights a week, four weeks a month. In fact, I preached it for about a year and a half and never once did I preach without feeling the anointing. The title was "He Is My Brother." It was a compassionate, emotional message which said, in essence, that these are not undesirables or bums, they are our brothers. They are people who need help.

At the end of my message I made a big play on the fact that you could ask me any question and I could answer it. Of course, I laughed and added that an answer could be, "I don't know." At one place a man jumped up and said very belligerently, "Isn't that a lot of money to spend on a kid?" Before I could answer, someone else jumped up and said, "Yes, that is a lot of money, unless it is my kid. On your kid it is a risky investment. On my kid, it's cheap." Of course, I told that story everywhere I went, and I discovered that people were not only willing, they were eager to give.

The Youth Redemption program was a good idea, but we had several problems. First, we were going into business when those who had blazed the trail were about to go out. Second, and more importantly, our facility was not in an ideal location. It was a beautiful facility—a former NIKE missile site—but it was on the outskirts of Lincoln, Nebraska, a desolate spot where the wind seems to howl off the prairie at twenty miles an hour year round. It was unrealistic to think that we could successfully transplant streetwise kids from New York or Philadelphia to such an isolated site.

Eventually, we phased out the drug ministry, and replaced it with Truth for Youth Crusades. The Crusades were designed to move into a city with an extended outreach to unsaved youth, then funnel them into local churches. The concept was fantastic and I found that people were as eager to support Truth for Youth as they had been Youth Redemption.

In one service people were packed even into the basement which was being used for the overflow. They heard the message over loudspeakers and when the offering time came, they rushed up from downstairs, pushed their way forward as far as they could, and threw their money on the stage.

Our largest campaign was targeted at New York City, an area where UPC did not have much of a foothold. We spent somewhere around $75,000 to $100,000 and before that we had seldom spent more than a few thousand on this type of project. Some of the promotions I dreamed up were used for years by everybody else for their own projects. For example, I had read an article in *Reader's Digest* about a blind boy who liked to run. He called his jogging "racing the wind," because he liked to feel the wind in his face when he ran. I suggested we call our New York campaign, "Racing the Rapture to N.Y.C." It was our challenge to get to New York and reach unsaved youth before the rapture. After that, everybody was "racing the rapture" to accomplish their pet projects.

I was flying everywhere to promote Truth for Youth and sometimes my boss, Donald Deck, accompanied me. On one trip we were hurriedly checking into the airport, and, to speed things along, Deck decided to take charge. I have to speak slowly to make my articulation clear, so every time the clerk asked me a question, Deck jumped in and gave the answer. I knew he was just trying to be helpful, so I let it pass. But when it came time to sign our credit card slips, the agent handed Deck my card and asked him to sign for me. When he realized what he had done, he cackled.

It didn't take us long to realize that we had different strengths and liabilities when it came to traveling. If we were shipping material and were a few pounds over the limit, Deck would go to the counter, demand to see the manager, tell him how many executives we had using their airline, how much money we spent with them a year, and so on, and generally create a scene. I could give $2 to the porter and ship 300 pounds over my limit. We learned to let me handle the baggage, bellboys and room service.

There were some things that no amount of money, ingenuity or effort on my part could make any easier, however. At headquarters I was required to write periodic reports and present them to the General Youth Committee. My first report was about two pages long and I was terrified. Obviously, I have no trouble speaking in front of a group, but because of my breathing problems, I am a horrible oral reader.

There I was, in front of fifty men trying to read two single-spaced pages, knowing to begin with that I can't read aloud, and also knowing that my nervousness was going to make it worse. My boss was very protective of me and all the men in the room were friends, so they were trying their best not to laugh. But when I finally got through, Deck could not contain himself any longer. He broke out in a belly laugh. Soon the whole place was laughing. I laughed along with them, but inside I felt the familiar aching humiliation. Here I was, in my mind, a guy who could raise a couple of hundred thousand dollars in a year and still couldn't read.

After Truth for Youth was launched and running smoothly, Deck occasionally asked me to take on a project or a trip that he needed help with. One year he agreed to attend a conference in London, then changed his mind at the last minute and sent me. Ordinarily, I would have been excited, but he gave me so little notice we didn't have time to get a passport and arrange for Gwenelda to go.

The conference started the last week of December and ended on New Year's Day. Since I couldn't get a direct flight home, I made stops in Paris and Berlin. I was never more lonesome in my life than I was in Berlin on New Year's Day with all the shops closed and Gwen half a world away. I ate by myself in the hotel dining room, then wandered around the city. I finally found one shop that was open and I bought Gwenelda a cuckoo clock. I had them wrap it in a crystal box because I knew Gwen didn't care anything about crystal and I wanted it to be a surprise. I wound up in the wee hours of the morning listening to the Rose Bowl on the Armed Forces Radio Network.

I got home the next day about 9 P.M. St. Louis time. I was

tired but we went to dinner at the finest Italian restaurant in St. Louis, maybe the world. After we finished eating, I gave Gwenelda her present. When she saw the crystal box, she pretended to be real excited, but I knew she was faking it. However, she was genuinely thrilled when she opened it and found the cuckoo clock inside.

I think I enjoyed the benefits from St. Louis more than my family did. Gwen had to become all things to the Oggs clan—mother, electrician, cook, counselor, disciplinarian. She did it all. Allan was at the age when he really needed me to be home more. He thought he was a lot bigger than he really was and consequently, he and I had a couple of confrontations.

I got home one time after being away for a few days and my wife met me with a concerned look on her face. She explained she was having problems with Allan and said, "I hate to admit it, but I can't do it anymore. I can't handle him. I felt he needed to be spanked and I spanked him with everything I had, and he didn't shed a tear. He just stood there, and when I was through he looked at me as if to say, 'Mom, do you feel better?' He really deserved to be punished and there was a spirit or attitude there that needed to be broken but I couldn't do it."

I kind of smirked a bit. If he was at a difficult age, so was I. He was fifteen going on twenty-three and I was thirty-eight trying to prove I was the same as twenty-one. It was an explosive combination. I was as big a problem for him as he was for me. When Gwen said she couldn't handle him, I smirked. She added, "Let me tell you something, I'm not sure you can either. He's a pretty big boy now."

When she said that, my problem got all mixed up with his. I said, "What do you mean? Do you really think that kid can handle me?" She said, "Be careful." I said, "Go get him."

The poor guy was asleep. He came out of his room expecting a gift, as I usually brought home bunches. He came stumbling out in a drowsy, half-conscious state, and I said, "You've had it now." He said, "Dad, when did you get home?" I said, "Don't talk back to me. Your mom tells me you need to get whipped and I want you to know I can do it." The poor kid wasn't quite awake yet and he said, "O.K., Dad." I said, "Go to your room and wait for me."

He went in his room and I used the flat of my hand. I spanked him like he was about four and a half years old and when I got through he just looked up as if to say, "Is that all you've got?" By now he was wide awake and he realized that all this was happening because of what he had done that day. But I was still pumped up. I had used my hand and that hadn't worked, so I took off my belt and I laid it on him. After all that, he looked at me again as if to say, "Dad, is that it?" And I said, "No, I've got more."

I look back on that night and I thank God for his grace and mercy. By then I had begun to realize there was something here that needed to be broken. Allan needed some help. We were face to face and something had to give and I got scared. Not afraid of him, but afraid for our future. He stood dry-eyed and a little confused, and I remembered that some of his friends had just left home, run away and not come back. I didn't want that to happen. I felt like I was walking a fine line.

I looked at him and said, "Allan, that's not all I have; there's something else I can do." He looked at me and said, "Dad, there's nothing else left. Mama's whipped me, you've whipped me, there's nothing left." And I said, "Oh, yes there is. Get on your feet and take your shirt off if you like. Get in your best position. If you think you are that big and tough, put up your dukes and let's fight man to man." He said, "Let's do what?" I said, "Let's fight. Put up your dukes and defend yourself 'cause I'm going to bust your nose right now." He looked at me so confused and I said, "Come on, son, let's go." He said, "You want me to fight you?" I said, "Well, you think you are so big and tough, man to man, let's go."

And when I said that, that big old boy's lip began to shake and his eyes filled with tears. He put both hands in his pj's—I'll never forget it—and stuck his chin out right at my fist and said, "Dad, here it is, you ought to hit it. Hit it all you want to."

He started crying and he said, "I want you to know I won't lift a hand against you now or ever. I'm sorry, I'm sorry. I deserve it. Work me over real good." He stood there limp and cried, and so did I. Remembering it now I must say, "Dear God, only by your grace, by your power, by your mercy, did that night somehow turn around to be a night of victory."

I left the room and crawled into the living room. I was so exhausted, I sat in my big chair and closed my eyes to kind of catch my breath. While I sat there with my eyes closed I felt something real heavy pressing on my lap, and when I opened my eyes, Allan was sitting on my lap telling me how much he loved me and I was telling him how much I loved him. In fact, on the phone this week before I hung up he said, "Dad, I love you," and I said, "Son, I love you." He is now twenty-seven years old. You see, the ingredient your home needs most is the same thing that mine needs: it's the presence of God and the love he alone can bring.

Another time I was coming home from a trip and as I drove into the driveway I could hear Gwen. When she gets angry, she can really get heated up. Allan was about sixteen then. I could tell as I approached the house that he had been disrespectful to her in some way and she was letting him know about it. She has, what we call, the "famous finger," and when she starts pointing it, you know you've had it. She had Allan backed against the kitchen wall and was putting the finger on him.

When I got into the kitchen, she turned on me like her neck was on a pivot and said, "Well, what are you going to do?" I didn't have all the details, but I had picked up enough to know that Allan had been rude to her, so I said, "I'll show you what I'm going to do."

She moved aside and I started in on Allan. I tried to slap him, but he was always like an octopus with his arms flailing everywhere. By the time my hand ricocheted off his arms, elbows, and hit his face, it wasn't much of a blow. We sometimes boxed with each other in the basement and would put on quite a show, going at it pretty hard, but this was nothing. However, I must have hit his nose at just the right angle, because all of a sudden there was blood everywhere.

Well, when that happened, my wife turned on me. She said, "Stop it! I didn't want you to kill him!" That quick, I had my wife, my mother, and the two girls standing there screaming at me and warning that I was killing him. Well, I wasn't about to kill him, I had just barely hit him. So I turned on them and said, "All of you, go to your rooms, *now!*" I think the psychology of blood was in my favor. They fled down the hall, with Allan running after yelling, "I'm O.K. I'm O.K."

That was a pretty hot scene, but about two hours later it was dinner time and we all sat at the same table and had a good meal. Before the meal was over we got loose, and started laughing about the whole thing. Of course, everybody was sorry for what had happened. But the reason we could sit down together at dinner was because, although we had problems, we were a family. We were Oggs . . . nobody wanted to change his name to Smith.

The worst crisis with Allan came when he decided to elope with his girlfriend. We came home one night and found him gone. As funny as it sounds, even though there was nobody home, he had climbed out the window. I went across town to his girlfriend's house and found him there. I brought Allan home, then we all sat down on the living room floor and started talking. Allan told me that he didn't have the Holy Ghost, he never had had the Holy Ghost, and that he wasn't that interested in church. He said, "I don't want to hurt you, Dad, but I don't feel anything, never have felt anything. I love you, but I want to go my own way." We talked for quite a while and I tried to back him down but he stuck to his guns.

I was scheduled to preach the Western District camp meeting in California, and we planned to fly to San Francisco and stay a few days then go on to camp. I had not discussed it with Gwen, but as we were sitting there, I suddenly said, "Well, I'll tell you what we're going to do. Instead of us flying to the camp, we're all going together and I want to leave as soon as possible." My wife said, "The laundry's not even done." I said, "Take it dirty." So within hours she had bundled up the laundry in sheets and tied it at four corners, loaded up the car, and we left.

Allan didn't want to go. He sat in a corner and fussed and grumbled and fought with his sisters. I was scared. I was afraid that at a gas stop or a restaurant he would split and I didn't want that. He had several friends in the church who had done that. I watched him like a hawk. We drove nonstop except for gas and food for twenty-four hours. I wanted to get as much distance behind us as I could the first day.

We stopped for the night early the next day. The girls did the wash. Then it kinda got to being fun. I realize now we shouldn't have done it. We wanted to cook in our room and the motel circuit breaker kept breaking. That was the first thaw in Allan. He went down and found the breaker box. He stood there and every time his mom would blow a fuse she'd wave and he'd flip the breaker switch.

Then we started loafing, driving from three to four hundred miles a day. By the time we got to camp, Allan had thawed real well. He met the young people at camp, dated a girl, and so on. When that camp closed, I was scheduled to preach another on Tuesday in Tennessee. I had an aunt who lived in San Francisco, so Gwen and the kids drove there and I flew to Tennessee. The idea was that they'd drive home together, I'd preach the second camp, and meet them in St. Louis.

About my second day in Tennessee, I got a long distance call from Wyoming. The car had broken down and Allan had had to hitchhike for miles to find a mechanic. There they were, stranded and absolutely miserable, yet I think it cost them $4 to get the car fixed. They weren't too far from Denver, so I told them to go to Denver. I would call my good friends, the Parkers, and preach for him on Sunday. I closed in Tennessee on Friday and flew to Denver. The whole family was fine.

In the Denver church there was a wealthy couple who

loved the pastor like a son. They had a palatial home and compound in the Rockies and they loved to share it. While I was sitting on the platform, I leaned over to the pastor and asked if he thought I could use one of their cabins for a few days. So we went to the Rockies, two miles from Rocky Mountain National Park. We stayed five days. We rode horses and camped and stayed in a lovely cabin. From there we drove home. The whole trip took thirty days and we were more of a family unit than we had ever been. From that summer till now, individual members may have had their problems, but as a family never. We are very close. That trip became known, with great affection, as "our family camp."

After I had been in St. Louis about three years, the directors of Youth Redemption and Truth for Youth Crusade called me in one morning and said, "You are doing a fantastic job! You are a fantastic preacher, you are a fantastic promoter . . . but the project is over." Although they gave me six months' notice that their ministries were being phased out, I was shattered by the decision. It found me at the threshold of my fortieth birthday, which made it even worse.

When I went to St. Louis, I thought I had arrived—that all the years of uncertainty and struggle were finally over. Now once again, at forty, I had no job and no place to go. While headquarters was still paying my expenses, I lined up as many preaching assignments as I could, put the word out that I was looking for a job or a church to pastor, waited . . . and prayed.

12

Going to Gainesville

WHEN MY WIFE AND I WENT to Gainesville, Florida, to investigate the possibility of my becoming pastor of the church there, Gwen was so apprehensive that she became ill. She felt like her nest had finally become secure in St. Louis and now things were being shaken. The kids were in a good private school, we had a nice home. There were a couple of possibilities I could pursue and perhaps stay in St. Louis. She said, "I'll go with you to Gainesville to meet these people, but I think we should stay here."

By the time we arrived in Gainesville, she was really sick. One of the ladies from the church, Sharon Teston, met us at the airport, and took us to her lovely home. Within hours Gwen had me in the corner of the bedroom showing me on paper all the reasons why we should move to Gainesville.

We bought a 3200 sq. foot, old colonial home in what was called the Duck Pond area. Forty years ago it had been the elite area of the city. It was now a historical district. We bought the place for a song. It was a beautiful home but it needed lots of work. When we bought it they backed up trucks to the windows and hauled off the trash. I worked on it steadily for about four years. After that, I got tired of working on it. By then, I had spent thousands of dollars, so we sold it and moved into a home that the church owned. It wasn't as nice or as big, but it appealed to us. The old house had eleven-foot ceilings and if I could have put $50,000 more into it, we would have had a quarter-million-dollar home. But I sold it for almost three times what I paid for it, so I got all my money and labor back, plus the fun I had doing it.

The church in Gainesville was the most understanding church I ever pastored. The people were wonderful. Their demands were very few. They wanted a good pastor, one who took care of their children, their sick, their elderly; they wanted good sermons; and they wanted to be givers. They did everything they could to make me happy. I had hours of every day that they didn't expect me to do anything unless an emergency came up. We had a two-car garage which I turned into a shop. Above that we had an apartment which we rented. When Allan and Cheryl got married they lived in it for a couple of months. It was a luxury home. The woodwork in it, compared to what's in homes today, would take your breath away.

The church folks helped us a lot. On different occasions, instead of giving gifts to us, they would do something for the house. It might be renovating the kitchen, or hanging wallpaper. I went off one day and when I came back they had all the floors downstairs refinished. They had pulled up all the old, stained carpet and they sanded down the floors to their original finish. It was simply beautiful. You could see your image mirrored in it. I spent hours almost every day working in my shop and barbecuing. I thought I had found my place forever.

Several incidents occurred in Gainesville which illustrate the interesting things you have to deal with as a pastor.

I taught a Bible lesson one Wednesday night on the sin that can so easily beset us. I titled it, "Everybody Has One." I didn't think that was a particularly suggestive title. After the service a lady who had been attending church for a couple of weeks asked to see me. That's not especially unusual so I said O.K. She came into my office, sat down and said, "I enjoyed your lesson very much. I'm new to your church and I have a problem. Like you taught tonight, I have a sin that could easily beset me." She was sitting there relaxed, with her legs crossed, very comfortably. She said, "God has given me a tremendous capacity for love."

I thought, O *no, here it comes.* I said, "Oh?" She said, "Yes." I said, "What do you mean?" She said "Well, my husband doesn't realize it but God has gifted me with more love than he can contain. For years I've just kinda shared myself with those who need attention and so forth." I thought maybe she was going to tell me there was someone in the church she was having an affair with. So I said, "Really? Who would you share yourself with?" She said, "Oh, anyone. People I'd meet at the Post Office, the laundromat." I said, "Well, how about here at the church? Is there anyone here you are attracted to?" She said, "O yes." I thought, *This is it.* I said, "Who?" She said, "There are several, even you."

When she said that I jumped up, opened my door and said, "I want to see you here Sunday night after service." When she came back Sunday night, I had my secretary acting as stenographer, along with the church board, and I explained to her what she could do, what she couldn't, where she could sit, what she could participate in. She was so casual. She talked about picking up men like she was buying candy or shoes. It was as if she had made that her spiritual gift.

Then one of the most unusual things I ever experienced happened to me. One Sunday afternoon we were taking a nap and the phone rang. My wife answered and I was just kinda listening in. It was a stranger calling to see if she could make an appointment to see me the next day. My wife said, of course. So at 2 P.M. Monday I went to the church and I saw a car in the parking lot. I went to my office to unlock the door.

When I got to the door it was unlocked but it wasn't

open. That was very strange, because I had broken the vacuum lock on it so that I had to open it and lock it with a key. Whenever I forgot to lock it it would open by itself. A time or two the police had called me and they would sit in my office and wait for me to come back and lock the door. There was no way the door could be unlocked and remain closed.

I walked in and there was a strange lady and her daughter. She said, "Before you say a word, Reverend, read this note." The note read, "My daughter's name is Sara. She was born with a severe birth injury. The doctor said she would never walk, talk or see."

That was identical to what the doctors had said about me. So I read the note and acknowledged that I understood what it said and I asked, "What can I do to help you?" She said, "I don't know." I said, "Well, where did you get my name?" Because the girl's condition was exactly like mine was supposed to be, it was like reading my own story. She didn't answer. I said, "Well, why are you here?" She just sat there and looked at me and said, "I don't know."

I said, "Would you like me to pray for Sara?" She said, "I've never been to a Pentecostal church, I've never spoken to a Pentecostal pastor, I'm frightened." I said, "There's no need to be frightened. In just a moment I'm going to get up and walk around my desk and lay my hands on your little girl and pray for her. I have cerebral palsy and my hand might quiver but don't let that alarm you."

Now when I had entered the office, to keep the door closed, I had locked it and I had left the key in the lock. I walked around the desk and prayed for the little girl. When I finished, the woman grabbed her daughter by the hand and dove for that door. She was turning the key so hard it was about to break. I grabbed the key and said, "What's wrong? I'll unlock the door. Who are you? What do you want? Why did you come? What can I do?" She looked at me and smiled real big then reached up and kissed my cheek. I unlocked the door and all she said was, "I just thought it was time for a miracle." Then she walked out.

I paused for about five seconds and I thought, *I need to know more about this.* I looked out the door and she was gone. There was no sign of her anywhere and her car had vanished from the parking lot. I got in my car and circled the block but everyone was gone. The only thing she left with me was the words, "I just thought it was time for a miracle." I never heard another word from her. Could she have been a part of the miracle—an angel?

For weeks I conducted my duties as if I entertained a heavenly messenger, an angelic being. I preached and taught, prayed for the sick and visited hospitals for months thinking, *It's time for a miracle.*

Another incident that occurred while I was in Gainesville had a less positive outcome. A young man whom I didn't know well was a state youth president. At a general conference he would excuse himself from board meetings or committee meetings, be gone half a day and come back. It turned out he was having an affair. He left his wife, but they eventually got back together and moved to Gainesville to build an independent Pentecostal church. He did everything he could to siphon off our members. I didn't fool with him. I just figured if he could outdo me, more power to him. My philosophy has always been, if you can out-hustle me, help yourself, but I don't think you can. I told Gwen, "When they give up, they'll come here."

They lasted about six months, and sure enough one Saturday morning he called and asked if he could talk to me. It was one of the saddest things I ever witnessed. Here was a man who had pastored a church, had been a state official with real finesse. A tremendous young man. And he sat at the table in tears and told me that he realized his challenge now was to save his soul, but that as far as the ministry went, he was through. Could he attend my church and would I pastor him and his family? I said of course I would.

"What you tried to do with the independent church doesn't mean a thing to me. And as far as anything else you did, why you did it or how, I could care less," I told him. "If you want to come, I'll pastor you as of this day. And if your little girl steals toilet tissue from the bathroom, I won't blame that on what you've done."

He was so appreciative. It was touching to pastor him and watch him adjust to the reversal in his life. He'd call me some nights at 11 P.M. to see if I wanted a cup of coffee. I knew he wanted to talk, so I would get dressed and meet him and he would talk for hours. He told me something one night that I've never forgotten.

He said, "Do you realize that every night when I go to bed, just before I go to sleep I hear ringing in my ear, 'You are a painter.' When I wake up in the morning, I know all my pastor friends are sleeping a little later and they get up and read their paper and then start their day. When I wake up in the morning, my feet hit the floor and my first thought is, 'I'm not a preacher, I'm a painter.'"

And that fellow lived with that every day of his life. It wasn't that he thought there was anything wrong with being a painter. He could have been a carpenter, a plumber or anything, but he lived with the sour taste of knowing that he was not now, nor ever would be, a preacher again.

He came on in the church and did well. He led some of the services and sang in a trio, but every week I'd give him personal attention, sometimes two or three times. He got up in one Wednesday night service and shared how grateful he was to be back in the church and about the wrong he had done. This was not necessary because everyone knew, but he felt he should do it. He turned his wife and two little girls inside out. But I think he kinda felt like the church wanted him to do that, to come clean. So I told him after the service, "Thank you for your testimony and we all heard it and no one here that I know of would need to hear it again." His little girls were just torn up. He didn't stay in the church a year after I left.

After that experience, when I went to Jackson College of Ministry, I tried to teach very plainly and definitely that for the pleasures of just a few moments you can kiss away fifty years of ministering. Sometimes one mistake can wipe out years of service.

As a pastor there are some things I can do easily, such as preaching, and there are others that I am still, after all these years, uncomfortable doing because of my handicap. But I have always done whatever I was expected to do, whether they were difficult or not. Hospital calls are one example. My bedside manner is good from the chin up. I have a lot of warmth, I love people, and I'm sincerely concerned about them. But I'd like to touch people. Sometimes there's nothing more valuable in all the world than to hold a hand. But there's no way I can or at least I don't think I can because of the way my hand shakes. I probably could and the shaking wouldn't surprise or bother them.

Another example is weddings. From the head up, I do as good a job as anybody at a wedding. I enjoy weddings. But at a wedding, traditionally, there's no podium. I have to have at least a lectern, and that's not a whole lot to hold on to. So, I've got my arm swinging. I try to hold it down, so that it isn't subtracting from what I'm saying (or at least I think it is). What I've got to say is beautiful but often I am thinking about my arm, my tightness, my awkwardness, worrying that it is detracting from what I want to say. I sometimes want to give my notes to the groom and say, "Here, you read it," because I've put time into it and I want people to be happy, to have their day without flaws. I like to do weddings and make people happy.

Many pastors don't do their own baptizing, but I've always done mine. It's not always a smooth shot. But I've always thought there was value in the candidate remembering that his pastor baptized him. There again, I can say everything right, but I can't hold the person's hand and the back of his neck, while I'm talking, because I would be in that position too long. So I do all my talking, then in one quick motion I baptize them. If I do it fast there's no problem. If they're not ready, they better get ready! I know the graceful way. I've seen people do it picture perfect. Well, I can't do it picture perfect. I could have nineteen reasons why Brother Oscar should do my baptizing and everyone would understand, but I have never done that.

I don't want people to die, but I love to preach funerals because to me they present a beautiful opportunity to express to people your love.

Gainesville was a tremendous experience. The five years we spent there might be described as "the best of times, and the worst of times." The first two years were an oasis for us. I don't think we ever received more warmth and love from a congregation. But at the end of those two years we began experiencing a series of personal crises that tested our entire family.

With Congressman Fuequa, Gainesville, Florida, for the church's "Happy Birthday, America" celebration, 1976

13

Landry, If You Could See Me Now

ONE JANUARY AFTERNOON, in my second year at Gainesville, I was playing racquetball, staying in shape so I wouldn't have a heart attack. I hit the ball and something struck me in my chest. I thought I was just out of shape. I left the court and walked around with this real bad pain. After a few minutes, it let up. I went back inside and said, "O.K., I'm ready." When I returned the first serve, the pain struck me again. My arms went numb and I had sense enough to know that I was in trouble. I left the court and walked two blocks, staggering in pain. I got to my car and drove home. I didn't want to scare my wife by calling her from the hospital.

I walked in the house and she was in the shower. I said, "Honey, I don't want to frighten you, but I'm going to the hospital and I thought maybe you'd go with me. I need you." She took one look at me and got dressed. While she was dressing, I went out to the car, and was blowing the horn.

When we got to the hospital, I found a nurse, tapped her on the shoulder and said, "Excuse me, but I need help bad. I am right now having a heart attack."

They grabbed me and scooted me off. In no time I had help everywhere. The pain was making me feel foolish. I was already beginning to feel depressed and despondent, because of the medication they were giving me. As they moved me to ICU, with my peripheral vision I tried to see Gwen, but I couldn't. I said, "Would you please stop?" but they just kept pushing the bed. I said, "Would you please wait?" but they kept on pushing. A big ol' boy from the church reached out and grabbed one of them and said, "The pastor asked you to wait!" They stopped and I asked, "Where's Gwen?" I was scared, I was hurting. I didn't know if there would be a future or how long it would be, or what adjustments I might have to make. I didn't know they had already told my family that I would probably not make it through the night.

Gwen said, "Here I am." I said, "I don't want to go one more foot without your promising me one thing!" Naturally she was upset but she said, "You name it, I'll do it." I said, "I want you to watch this bunch. Don't take your eyes off them. Don't let them give me anything that would take away the preacher." She smiled. I said, "Don't smile, don't laugh at me. I'm serious. Don't let them probe around in there and give me years to live without being able to preach. Don't let them get my preacher!" She said, "I pledge to you I'll watch them."

Everybody else in ICU had visitors fifteen minutes every couple of hours or so. Gwen was allowed to stay by me twenty-four hours a day. She had to sneak away from me to go to the bathroom. My thinking was crazy. From 4 to 9 P.M. I was in incredible pain. But I fooled the whole bunch. I lived. Many preachers and friends called to encourage Gwen. But one man called to ask who they should contact about the church. When she said, "Well, contact the pastor," the man replied, "But he's dead." (Not quite!) They moved me from ICU to a monitored room, then finally to your regular million-dollar-a-day room.

One day as I was lying there, I still wondered about the preacher, *Did I lose it? Did somebody get it?* I asked the nurse, "Would you just close the door and leave me alone for awhile?" The palms of my hands got sweaty. I was scared. I was going to probe around and find out if I could, if it was still there, if I still had the preacher. I started, "Jessie had a whole bunch of boys . . ." and I just began telling the story of David and Goliath. You couldn't get more basic. I was digging around trying to see if I had it. I said, "And Goliath growled like a dog and a little boy came out and passed over a brook and went to picking out some stones. The water was rippling over the stones. . . ." When I said, "rippling," I felt something ripple all through my body. My heart felt like it had never pumped stronger. I made the altar call right there. I didn't go any further. With tears trickling down my face, I cried, "I got it, I got it, I got it."

After I came home, I was very nervous. It didn't take much to upset me. Anything emotional would trigger tears. That was the result of the surgery. You go through the "weeps." You cry about everything. Somebody hits a home run and you cry because he's such a good boy. You're very frightened about your future. In fact, you think it's gone. You get the idea that you are not as much a man as you were before. When you start walking, you can't make it to the corner. Time changes all that but you think, *Man, last week I was playing racquetball and now I can't walk to the car*. It is very difficult.

Fortunately, our bedroom was large and had its own sitting room and bath so I could go there and let the whole world go by. My wife brought me my meals and I didn't have to fool with all the hustle.

Among themselves, my family and the church folks decided to isolate me from all problems. Actually, the church had been remarkably free of trouble. Ironically, the biggest problem we ever had with the church occurred during this recuperation period and arose out of an attempt on the part of the congregation to do something nice for me. They had decided to re-do our kitchen and breakfast nook, but they couldn't agree on how the work should be done. Part of the church wanted to do the labor themselves, others thought it should be contracted out. This seeming molehill quickly turned into a mountainous problem which split the church in two. However, I was oblivious to all of this—at least at first.

One young man in the church (he was a wonderful person, but very hyper) somehow got by all the security precautions Gwen had erected and came into my room. He sat down and said, "I know I'm not supposed to tell you this, but I've got to talk to somebody." Then he proceeded to tell me all about the war. Well, I was man enough not to let him see it upset me, but when he left, I went to pieces. Of course, Gwen picked up the pieces, and she was ready to take care of that young man once and for all. But Allan said he would handle it. He told two or three men in the church and they went to the young man. They were fellow Christians and tongue talkers, but they let him know that one time was the limit.

Because my assistant was not comfortable preaching in my pulpit, and because of the church split, I had to return to preaching sooner than I should have. I was still very weak. By the time I preached on Wednesday and twice on Sunday, I was shot. But the church realized that and I guess they appreciated my effort. It seemed like every Sunday night somebody would shake my hand, leave a chunk of money in it and say, "Brother Oggs, we want you to rest for the next couple of days." I spent many of my Mondays and Tuesdays on the beach and it never cost me a penny and it didn't come out of the church treasury. It wasn't hard to preach knowing I had a hotel waiting for me at the beach.

I was invited to speak at my second General Conference the October after I had my heart attack. They introduced me as a man who had been twice dead (at birth and at my heart attack) and twice resurrected.

I preached on Jonah, who had also experienced a sort of resurrection. For my title, I used Paul Harvey's by-line, "The

Rest of the Story." I had never realized who wrote the book of Jonah. When it dawned on me that Jonah wrote the book, I was amazed. That was the rest of the story. In spite of all the negatives in Jonah's life, he still had enough courage to write the story.

If most of us had been in Jonah's place, we would never have admitted that we were running from God when the storm hit the ship we were on. We would have been more likely to say, "I was on this ship when a bunch of drunken sailors, all stewed up, threw me overboard." But Jonah said, "I know what the problem is. I'm the problem. Throw me off."

We need to have the courage to look at ourselves honestly, as Jonah did. If we don't, we risk creating a lot of hurt and problems for ourselves and others. If anything positive came out of my "belly" experience, it was that I gained greater insight into myself. Sometimes I could even admit that I was the problem. It is a lesson we all need, but I wouldn't recommend a heart attack as the best way to learn it!

During the time we were in Gainesville, Allan still represented quite a challenge. He was skipping school, sneaking around smoking and spending more time than his mother thought he should with girls. Some of them would even come by our house at night and throw rocks at his window. His grades were terrible and he finally dropped out of high school.

One day I sat down with him and asked, "Allan, have I been good to you?" He said, "Oh, yeh." "Have you ever asked me for anything that I didn't do my best to do it for you?" "No, Dad." "Well, I want to ask you one thing. I've given you my best for eighteen years. Would you give me one year?" "Yeh, O.K." "I want you to go to Apostolic Bible Institute. I know you didn't graduate, but I'm sure you could take the GED test and pass. Would you go there for just one year?" He said, "Dad, I'm not called to preach, but I owe that to you."

He was eighteen then. He went from sunny Florida to St. Paul, Minnesota. He'd call home in the winter months and say, "Mama, tell me about the sky, is it blue?" He didn't do well in school. His GPA was low, not quite a C. But he did work full time which he had never done before. He'd always had part-time jobs, but if he got tired of them or they wouldn't let him off for a date, he'd quit. The hardest subjects there were the ones he liked most and he made his best grades. The toughest teacher there was his favorite. But all the little, easy classes he didn't like and he flunked them. He wouldn't go to class, or he'd sleep through them.

Late in the year, the school sent me a letter telling me my son was not fit to attend their school and that he was expelled. That was a real blow. I couldn't imagine what he had done to deserve such drastic wording and action, especially with no warning. I called right away. Of course I knew everyone up there and I asked, "Would you do one thing for me? Don't send him home until I can get there."

I arrived about 9:30 that night. Allan was scared to death. They had a 10:30 meeting scheduled where he was to meet the entire faculty. They said I could go in with him. It was a little like the UN. We all sat around a table. He sat behind me and I pled his case for an hour.

I had just been there two months before and had not heard one negative comment. I had gone to every teacher there and none of them had said a critical word and now two months later they're telling me he has missed dozens of classes. The president was a friend of mine and strong as a lion. There wasn't a thing I could do but make my case and ask for mercy. Otherwise Allan was finished. When I finished, all but one man was in tears. The president, that hard-nosed old soldier, leaned up and said, "I have never heard such an appeal in my life." Allan was crying, I was in tears and the Spirit of God was everywhere. The president said, "Allan doesn't have to go, but he'll have to apologize publicly." Well, that was humiliating, but we agreed.

Overnight, I put two and two together and figured out what I went through was part of what was wrong. The school was also in the midst of a morale problem; Allan fell heir to the message, "We don't care who you are, you've got to line up."

When we got to the president's office the next morning, I said to the president, "Allan is prepared to read his apology, but I want to be there to give him my support. I'll just slip in and sit in the back." "O no," he said, "I want you to sit on the platform." I thought, *Man, you talk about overkill!* I said, "O.K." It was all starting to fall in place. I thought, *This is going to be interesting!*

Now, when the president introduced Allan, he told the rest of the student body if they had one negative comment to make about him, they would be sent home. Allan was about to make a statement that only a man could make. I thought, *You are using Allan being up here and me with him, to give the school a shot in the arm.* Allan read his statement. Then, with no warning, the president got up and said, "Allan's dad is a man of God, and now we'd like him to preach for us." My son had just been crucified. He stood there humiliated and I sat there wanting to cry. And now the president said, "Now we're going to hear from his daddy." I thought, *We are not going to let you make us look bad.*

So I got up and preached on "The Land of the Hesitator." Jonah and Simon Peter both hesitated, in the same city, to fulfill the will of God, although they did so several hundred years apart.

What do you think that did to Allan? For some time, it made him bitter. He thought, *Who needs the ministry?* He had done nothing immoral. Many of his teachers told me privately that they were sorry about what had happened to him, but there was nothing they could do. They added that if everyone who did what Allan had done had to apologize, we'd all still be in the auditorium.

I got letters for months after that from students thanking me for coming to the school to support Allan. Allan stuck it out for two years. Then he left and married a wonderful girl.

When we went to Gainesville, I really thought I would stay there until I retired. I loved the church. I loved the people.

I loved the city. I don't think I could ever pastor a church that would treat me any better. But by our fifth year, I began to feel restless.

One December evening, we were having dinner with some folks from the church and after we left I asked Gwen, just out of the clear blue, "Honey, do you think maybe we're through here?" She broke down crying and said, "That's it, we're gone!" I said, "No, I'm just talking. I don't have anyplace in mind. I'm just wondering if we've done all we can here."

I had some problems being challenged by a local church. I don't think anybody tended their sheep any better than I did, but others seemed to relish a local challenge more than I did. In UPC I was known as a preacher and a promoter. I could get more excited going to eight camps and eight District Conferences telling them about Truth for Youth or some other program, than I could plotting how to increase a Sunday school twelve percent over the long haul.

I have wondered at times, what would have happened if I had channeled all my energies into a local church—if I had stayed in Gainesville or someplace else. I have pastor friends who can say with pride that they have a home, two cars, a boat and 300 in their congregation. I ask them, "But where have you been?" I am just as proud and excited to say that I have preached in 1,000 or 1,500 places in 30 years. I can be laid off or fired and never miss a day's preaching.

We had other personal reasons for considering leaving Gainesville. By the time we left, Gwenelda was almost relieved. Debra had gotten married and was very unhappy. She was living just a few blocks away and it was difficult to be that close, seeing all her dreams and ours for her drying up. Her husband made it very difficult for us all. We had to just ignore some of the obvious problems, such as the fact that he could be so unkind to her.

We never really discovered what happened. They left on their honeymoon joyous, like all newlyweds, but they came back different. When they got back, Debra was not allowed to be herself. As close a family as we are, that was devastating, and things went from bad to worse every day. That was a real factor in our leaving. We figured if we got away, it might help. As it turned out, they followed us to Jackson and moved in with us, while he went to Jackson College of Ministry free.

We were sitting on our bedroom balcony one night, trying to get away from them, because we could hear them fighting. Again he became abusive. Now when Gwen gets angry, she is like Machine-gun Kelly. She was up on her feet and off the balcony so fast, he knew he had trouble. I followed. As usual I got all tightened up and ready to fight, but I couldn't do anything. It was like when I was a boy. I'd have to get hit a few times before I could loosen up enough to fight back. I just stood there while I thought of all the things I'd like to do to him. After that, he left and that was the end. He came back once when we were gone, broke the door down, took his stuff and some of mine and left.

Before they were married, he was very congenial. I really think he thought I had more money than I do and that he believed the ministry would be easier to break into than it is. I think he thought that with my help he would soon be driving a new car and flying out to speak twice a week like I was. However, he forgot that my flights were many days getting off the ground.

Before we left Gainesville, we did have one other outstanding experience. I was in Bossier City, Louisiana, preaching one Sunday morning when the phone rang and Gwen told me she had just found out that Allan's wife, Cheryl, was pregnant. When I heard it, I popped my buttons. It was no big deal, but it said to me, "Here I am handicapped yet I have come full circle. Now what is left that I wasn't supposed to do or what is left that a person, anybody does, that I haven't done?" It instantly made me feel that for a person who wasn't supposed to have much of anything, I hadn't missed much. I preached up a storm that morning because I was a prospective grandpa. I told the whole church.

Clint was born on Christmas day and that was a happy occasion. My wife burned the whole meal. We had all kinds of company coming that day and she burned everything. She didn't tell me. After we had eaten she asked me how I liked it. I said fine. She asked me if I noticed anything different and I said no. She told me then that she had had the whole meal catered. We were so happy. Too bad you can't have *grand* kids first—they are so much easier and more fun!

Clint's birth did something special for Allan. It was remarkable. Before the baby came, Allan loved Cheryl, but he was still groping with who he was and what he wanted. But when the baby came, instantly there was one thing he knew: he was a father! That mantle rested on his shoulders immediately. And from day one he knew as much, if not more, about the baby than Cheryl.

Things are coming back around now. Just a few months ago Clint began understanding that his grandpa is crippled. Out of the clear blue sky he told his mama and daddy, "I know what is wrong with Grandpa. He walks funny." That's what you call full circle. First there was me, then there was Allan and now there's Clint, learning to cope with my handicap.

What did I lose by being handicapped? What did I miss? If a witness is required, now there are three generations. I wasn't a flash in the pan. I have lived a normal life. I know I may have left some fingerprints around so you could figure out that I was different, but I traveled the route. I made the journey and that is a tremendous feeling.

I don't think I was ever more aware of that than when I spoke to a Sunday School Convention for the entire state of Missouri. I was the featured speaker for three nights. Hundreds of people attended, including dozens of pastors, any one of whom would have felt honored to be in my place. Lanny Wolfe and his choir ministered in music. The place buzzed and hummed with excitement, and I was feeling "happy drunk" just to be there.

The first night the Holy Ghost fell. People were shouting,

running and worshiping. Everybody was on his feet crying, "Hallelujah, thank you, Jesus." As I watched the eruption of worship, I thought back to that night when a sixteen-year-old crippled boy got up in the pulpit with no notes and the Holy Ghost fell. Scenes of his life over the next thirty years began flashing through my mind. I watched as he struggled to overcome his handicap, and battled the doubts of others. I felt his discouragement and fatigue. And I shared his pride when success finally began to come his way.

I could stand it no longer. I got up and screamed at the top of my voice for a man named Landry—the man who had popped the top of his head and said, "You can't be a preacher." Everybody else was yelling, "Jesus, Jesus." I yelled, "Laaandry." Nobody heard me, it was too noisy.

The second time, I yelled, "Laaandry, are you here?"

The third time I yelled, "Laaandry, I wish you were here. If you were here, you would get to see us in action—me and the grace of God. I'm preaching tonight. I'm not coming anymore. I'm here!"

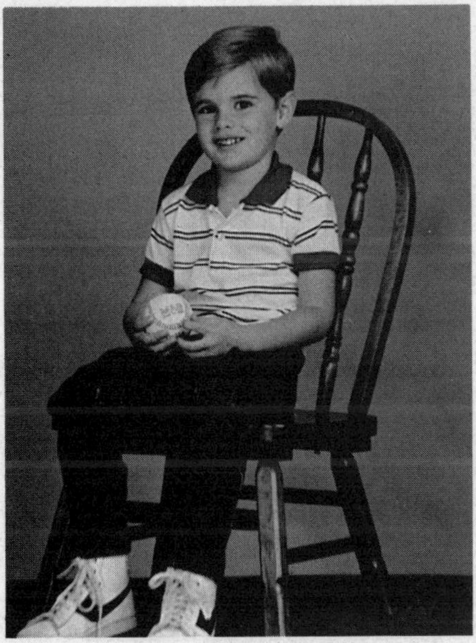

Clint Allan Oggs, grandson, 5

The whole clan (except Clint) in 1986

14

P.B. Who? Again

THE PRESIDENT OF JACKSON COLLEGE of Ministries called me at one in the afternoon to ask if I would serve on a pastors' advisory board to JCM. I thanked him, but explained that I was a member of the Board of Directors of another college, therefore I felt like I could not be involved with JCM.

After hanging up the phone, I told Gwen what the conversation was and she promptly informed me that she did not want me ever in the future to express what I thought needed to be done regarding our old alma mater, PBI, which had been renamed JCM. Her logic was, "When you can do something to help you won't, so when you can't do anything don't bother me with it." When my children came home she told them that I had turned down the president and they all agreed that I should involve myself with the old school.

Hence, that same day I was on a plane to Jackson, Mississippi. I wasn't there long before it was very obvious that there were some things that needed to be done and I could help. I was asked to put together a new promotional and public relations package. With the help of a commercial artist, Gilbert Davenport, of Royal Oak, Michigan, we set out to accomplish this very exciting goal.

A few months later at the National Music Ministers Conference, which was held at JCM, I learned that the executive vice-president of the college had resigned. I applied for the job. The President, Thomas L. Craft, came to my hotel room and I presented to him my interest in the position. A few months later I was happily involved in JCM.

I went to JCM for several reasons, the main one being that I wanted to teach homiletics. I did everything else the job required to have the opportunity to influence young men getting started in the ministry. It's not enough to have a head filled with knowledge and a heart enlarged with the Spirit and power of God. It must be communicated head to head and heart to heart.

I did all the paperwork and office duties just to be there when a young man would come in and say, "Brother Oggs, I've got this thought. What would be the best way to go from here?" It was pure joy to close the door and share with him. Then I'd wait for him to come back and tell me how it went. You pretty much knew how it went, but you'd sit and listen while he told you, and you'd divide what he said in half, but at that stage his enthusiasm was more important than anything he said.

Nothing could equal the satisfaction I felt when a young man from Omaha, Nebraska, Howie Tiller, talented, articulate, nice-looking, told me, "Finally, I know where I'm going, I know where I am and I understand where I have been. I am going to be a preacher of the gospel!"

After thirty-three years, I'm still in love with preaching. Preaching is God's plan to save the lost. Everything else is great—seminars, programs, teaching. But the Bible doesn't say teaching will save the lost. It says God chose preaching to save the lost.

Working with youth can also be funny. Like the time I was talking to a young man about his coming out of a dormitory window late at night and he said, "Whoever told you that is a liar. I'll put my hand on the Bible and call him a liar." I sat there thinking, *You idiot, what you don't know is that I was the one who watched you come out of the window.*

JCM also satisfied my need for a challenge. I realized how important that is to me one night in Marion, Illinois. I was in an airport, having dinner with a pastor. He was in his mid-forties and beginning to feel like life was passing him by. While we were talking, a plane landed and a lot of men came through the gate carrying briefcases. I said to him, "When I get off a plane, there will usually be several young men who get off with me. We all have suits, ties, and briefcases. We all look basically alike. But the young man bounces off the plane thinking, *I'm going after it.* I get off the plane, probably with more money in my pocket, but without the zest. The difference is that the young men are thinking, *If I don't get it today, I will tomorrow.* You and I have more, but feel less secure than they do, because they are pursuing. They are still tracking, sniffing, ambushing and shooting. We made the kill, but after you made it, all you've got left is to skin it and take the meat home."

JCM gave me an opportunity to keep tracking. It was similar to my experience in St. Louis. The school had serious problems when I arrived. A solid program had to be built. And then I had to rebuild confidence in the college. Since it drew students from all over the country, I had to do a lot of traveling. For me, JCM offered the best of both worlds. I had a national arena in which to practice my abilities, I got to travel, but I had the security of a salaried position. It was gratifying to see my efforts pay off, too. The enrollment climbed steadily, reaching an all-time high in 1984, and other schools began to copy our success.

Returning to JCM as vice president also had deep personal significance for me. The boy who everybody said could never be a preacher, the poor student who couldn't write, was now teaching preachers at his alma mater!

But the most gratifying experience I had at JCM was

handing a degree conferred by the college to our son, Allan. It had to be one of the greatest thrills of my life. Allan is now actively involved in full-time ministry.

I loved Jackson. The people there are warm and friendly, and the city has a quaint Southern charm. But I had a humiliating experience shortly after we arrived in town, which reminded me again that for a handicapped person, the struggle is never really over.

I went down to the state auto licensing bureau to get my driver's license renewed. I had carelessly allowed it to lapse, so now I had to take the driver's test again. Unfortunately, I got a hard-nosed cop, who took one look at me and said, "No way am I going to get in a car with you. You couldn't possibly pass the test." I was so humiliated, I practically crawled away. Then, I got angry. I got my first driver's license at sixteen, and this guy was telling me after thirty-two years that I couldn't drive!

I went straight to my doctor and asked him to sign a statement saying I was physically able to drive. By this time I was so furious that I blasted him. I got so upset that I began to feel weak and dizzy. I stopped at a coffee shop on the way home, thinking a cup of coffee and a doughnut with lots of sugar might help. But I didn't feel any better. I went home and laid down, and the room began spinning. I knew then that I was really sick, but nobody was at home. I began to get frightened. By the time Gwenelda came home, I couldn't move at all. Even turning my head made the whole room go crazy. She took one look at me and called an ambulance. By the time they arrived, I was vomiting and deathly ill.

I spent several hours in the emergency room, while they took all kinds of x-rays, cardiograms and tests. Finally, a doctor came in. He pulled a chair up next to my bed and asked, "Rev. Oggs, did anything upset you today?" He told me that the combination of anxiety and anger had created an imbalance in my inner ear that was causing my dizziness and nausea. The next day, I was fine. I took my doctor's certificate, passed the test with no problems and got my license. But I had put myself and my family through torment, all because someone had dared to suggest that I couldn't drive because I was handicapped!

Fortunately, not long after that, my handicap was displayed in a more positive setting. A tape of a sermon I had given several years earlier was played on Dr. James Dobson's radio program, "Focus on the Family." That broadcast rearranged all my plans. Out of nowhere this good man's ministry opened my thinking and initiated a completely new avenue of ministry for me. When I stood at the elevator with Dr. Dobson after meeting with him September 6, 1985, my parting words, based on and encouraged by his comments were: "I'm going to do it . . . I'm going to write a book."

I was so excited that I almost ran to my car, drove around the corner to a rather nice little Mexican restaurant and sat there making notes on a napkin for this autobiography, *You Gotta Have the Want-To.*

My plans ran into a major detour a month later, on October 21, 1985, when Dr. Kilgore showed me a diagram of all my occluded arteries, and expressed his professional opinion that I really needed to consider by-pass surgery. My future, he felt, would be very threatened if I did not do so. When he left the room I studied the diagram and then put it down on the bed and said to my wife, "It doesn't leave me much to work with." Then after a long pause, I added, "But I want to write my book."

I had gone to General Conference in early October. It was about a half-mile from my hotel to the convention center and I walked back and forth about a half-dozen times a day. It was no problem. I enjoyed it.

Thursday, I felt a soreness or tightness in the base of my neck. Friday when I walked, it was a little lower in my chest but it wasn't real bad. However, by Saturday or maybe Sunday it got so sore that I could only walk 100 feet or so before I'd have to stop to window shop. It got to my arm and by then I knew what it was but I kept on going. I was nearer to the convention center than to the hotel. When I got there, I met a man I hadn't seen in years. He took one look at me and asked what was wrong. I sat in the conference for about half an hour and decided there was no need to deny the pain, so I took a cab back to the hotel and went to bed.

The next day I went back and forth to the convention several times by cab. My wife was aware of the soreness. She called Debra and Debra called my doctor. So when I got home I had an appointment with him. We stayed over Monday thinking the rest would be good for me and I just slept all day. I got home Tuesday and went to my doctor. He immediately said I would need to see a cardiologist.

I went to him on Thursday and he checked me into the hospital on Sunday to do a heart catheterization. I took it on Monday and he came in to show me what the problem was. His name was Dr. Kilgore. In three of my arteries I had 100 percent occlusions plus several occlusions in the fourth artery. I had only 10 percent of the fourth not occluded. He recommended surgery and left the room.

When he left, Gwen and I were in a state of shock. She turned her head away from me and looked out the window. I looked at the picture. My first words to her were, "Baby, I really don't have much left." We both wept. Then my next comment was, "But I don't want to go. I want to write a book. I'm not ready. I have too much to do." She went home for a few hours and Tuesday the doctor came back. He was waiting for my decision.

I call this period getting my medical degree because I quizzed everybody about everything. I made them draw me pictures, diagrams, and graphs. Without the surgery they gave me a 25 percent chance of living 5 years. With the surgery it jumped to almost 97 percent. They told me the percentages of dying on the table. So when I got all the percentages, I said, "I'll let you know." I made up my mind when Gwen went home.

When she came back my first decision was to do it on Sunday. But when I woke up the next day, I knew within half an hour that was no good. I could see the waiting would drive me crazy. So I called her and said I wanted to do it as soon as I could. The doctor had told me he didn't have an opening on Wednesday, but suddenly he had a cancellation. So I said, "Let's do it."

He allowed me to check out on a furlough. So I went by the school and had lunch with everybody. I still had my hospital name tag on my wrist. I had one of the girls in the office pull the band up on my arm and tape it so it wouldn't show when I ate lunch. It was frightening. Cupit was there and of course, my children. The surgery was set for 2 P.M.

Before the surgery I quizzed every doctor except the anesthesiologist. I wanted to make sure he knew I had C.P. The best I got from him was a phone call. He said he wouldn't get to see me before surgery because he was baby-sitting. This guy's bill was the second highest! I met Kilgore's assistant first. He looked about thirty. I tried to be real polite, but as soon as he left, I told my wife, "There is no way that boy is cutting on me. You tell the office I want to see his daddy, not him." So Dr. Kilgore came back.

I asked him how many by-pass surgeries he had done. He said, "We have done at least 2,000." I said, "I didn't ask how many *we* did, how many have *you* done?" He said he'd done at least half of those so I felt pretty secure. I do remember dreaming, coming out of the anesthetic, that I died, and they told me that's normal. I dreamed that everybody around me was dying too.

When I get real weak, heart attack weak, my coordination is nothing. People in the recovery room were not aware of that. I asked them not even to try to put the IV in my right arm but they were determined that they would. Well, they poked around, and I can take pain pretty well, but they finally had to go to the other arm.

When I came out of the anesthetic they got me up and I guess they thought I was some kind of pampered CP person. I never say CP victim. I don't think I'm a victim of anything. So they got me up and put me in a chair and put some kind of liquid meal before me. Well, I couldn't handle it. I just absolutely couldn't handle it. But this woman was telling me, like a big therapeutic nurse, take care of yourself. To me that was so humiliating because I've always taken care of myself. I could write the book on "how." So I tried to tell her that I've always taken care of myself, but right now I just can't. Well, she left the room. But just about then, my wife came in and when she realized what had happened, she got hot. She was at it again—protecting me. She worked that nurse over good. Then she fed me.

When I had my first heart attack, my oldest girl Debra never left me. So this time she moved in again. My other girl, Jody, came and went and the second day I went back to my room. I ate everything they gave me. It was all garbage but I felt that if I didn't eat it I wouldn't get strong. As soon as I could think, I was in gear to get well.

When they said I could walk, it wasn't any time till I was exceeding what they told me I had to do. When they said walk, I took off pushing myself. You're just there for a week, and by the time I came home, I was covering the whole floor. I walked and walked. When they'd go to sleep, I'd walk. I had some thoughts of dying, but not a whole lot. One of my first goals was to get healthy—eat this junk and walk so I could have my family together at home for Christmas.

The day I got home I started walking. I began walking about a block a day and didn't miss a day ever. They give you a pre- and post-operation book. I studied the book. I could identify every pain. They had a walking schedule. I made every checkpoint. The book said that at the end of thirty days you should be up to two or three miles a day. So on the thirtieth day I reached my three miles. I went by the book.

Two weeks after the operation I went to see my internist. My wife drove me, and he said I could start driving again, and I could go back to work a couple of hours a day. I think he said that because the night before I visited him was the only time I had any serious depression. I hit the pits in the night.

It took me several hours but in the midst of my depression, after being sorry for myself for quite awhile, I came around and decided I needed to check out what was left and what I would like to do with it. So I just sat down and got to thinking what I thought I could still do. I decided I could still preach, I could still teach, and I could write a book. I located some things that if I lived one year or ten I would enjoy doing.

I did a lot of talking to myself . . . I recommend it. I decided, O.K., this is what you have left. Now what you ought to do is get real busy and beat this depression business. Even before daylight I had so talked myself out of depression I couldn't sleep because I was so excited. I was excited about writing and what this would open up for me.

I became very involved with my notes. The book could not have come at a better time. Even the deadline the publisher had given me for submitting an outline was good because it made me think I had to hustle. I went back to work and between my working two hours, resting, writing, and walking, I had a full day. I would be more than happy to go to bed at night. I had a few little dips of discouragement, but no real depression at all.

When I went to see Dr. Kilgore, I drove my car. I met one of his nurses in the downstairs lobby, waiting for the elevator. She asked, "Who drove you here?" I said, "I drove myself." When I went upstairs, the receptionist said, "Come on back, Rev. Oggs, and it will be O.K. for the person who brought you to come back too." And I said, "But nobody brought me." She was surprised. By then, I was feeling kinda proud of myself.

Before my heart attack in '76, I played racquetball two or three times a week, but I hadn't played in six or seven years. Now Dr. Kilgore told me that by June I could play again. Whether I ever played or not, just to know that I could was great. Of course I played!

Two months after my surgery, Gwenelda and I attended the annual faculty and staff Christmas party. The room was aglow from both a tree of lights and the presence of the Tree of

Life. President Craft expressed his amazement at my speedy recovery and said to Gwenelda, "Your husband should be wearing an 'I Am a Survivor' T-shirt."

Ruby Martin, who had been an instructor at JCM for forty years, and had taught me, spoke up and said, "If anybody thought you wouldn't be back real soon, they didn't know you or your fight record. You have been battling percentages all your life!"

The glow of good feeling that filled the room that night faded quickly in the New Year. It didn't seem possible, but once again, it rained on my parade. I lost my job at JCM. At fifty, once again I had to pull out my black book and start over.

J.C.M. Banquet, 1985

15

You Gotta Have the Want-To

AT THIRTY-FIVE, I THOUGHT THAT FIFTY would be a time to take it easy. I thought at fifty you would begin to taper. But on my way to fifty-one, I have experienced some of the lowest lows and the highest highs of my life.

After losing my job at JCM, I had to face some hard facts. I was neither young nor old, but I was nearer to being old than young. There was no reason I couldn't pastor a church again, but no one was beating down my door at this time asking me to come.

In our fellowship, I was known primarily for my promotional abilities and my preaching. I still had my black book, but I really didn't want to go back to full-time evangelizing. Traveling all over the country, preaching two or three nights at a time, was a grueling way to make a living and it no longer presented the challenge to me that it had twenty or even ten years ago.

I had a couple of offers, one of them very lucrative, to help other ministries with promotion, but I was getting a little tired of promoting other men's projects. As I had discovered twice now, it was not a very secure form of employment. I decided I was not going to put all those hours in again to support someone else's idea. For a change, I was going to give myself something that was mine. If I could get another man's dreams to flourish, perhaps I could my own.

After much thought and prayer, I decided to pursue one of my keen interests. For a long time, I had been concerned with the lack of any formal training in homiletics offered to UPC preachers. That was one of the reasons I had gone to JCM. So I decided I would move from the college scene to pastors and evangelists. I would hold seminars around the country for preachers interested in improving or brushing up their techniques. I would promote preaching.

My first job was to develop a curriculum for the seminars, then design brochures and materials I could send to pastors. Once again, my black book came in handy. Nothing like this had ever been done before in UPC and the initial response was encouraging. I was excited. I called my new venture "Pulpit Ministries," and I loved it!

At fifty-one, I am still overcoming those childhood hurts of always being chosen last. I still want to be first, not just to be first, but because for so long it hurt to be last. Even now, I have a certain amount of fear that if I'm not busy, it might be because I am not capable. I have a continuing need to get beyond the hurt. That is what makes my seminars so rewarding. That is why it is so fulfilling for me to have the opportunity to share in developing the ministry of hundreds of "in-the-field preachers" all over America. The seminar enrollment makes a loud statement about my preaching ability.

Before the end of the five-month grace period that JCM had given me, we left Jackson and moved "home" to Kenner. When we had said good-bye to Kenner fifteen years earlier,

Gwenelda had sworn she would never come back. I knew this move was hard on her and Jody.

Part of my joy in Jackson had been the affluence and stability I had been able to give them. I could say to Gwen, "Sure, Baby, if you want it, buy it." Not that she was extravagant. Mostly she bought things for the kids or new furniture for our townhouse. Now a lot of the furniture had to be stored while we moved into a small apartment again. Our income took a drastic drop, and I wondered if I could work hard enough to make up for the loss. I knew Gwenelda was scared to death about our finances, but she would never admit it. Out of her love and loyalty for me, she buried her worries.

Jody had graduated from high school just before we left Jackson. She had planned to go to college immediately, but now she was working in a department store, selling boy's clothing. She had put her college career on hold, taking just one course at a junior college in New Orleans, until she could meet the residency requirements to qualify for in-state tuition. She put up a brave front too. "I love living in New Orleans," she told me often. "It's a wonderful old city and the shopping and food are fantastic." But occasionally, when one of her friends from Jackson called, a crack appeared in her wall of bravado. She only fooled me when I wanted to be fooled.

One night as I was lying in bed trying to figure out what I could do to make more money, everything crashed in on me—Gwenelda, Jody, the hurts, the tremendous battles they had waged to protect me. For just a minute the thought flashed through my head—"everything would be so much better for them, if I weren't here." It didn't linger. I pushed it away before it had time to put down roots and become an idea. But for that instant I felt like, "I've had it. It's been long enough, this constant being in gear, always hustling and telling the whole world, 'I can, I can, I can!' I'm tired of fighting, tired of hurting."

As incredible as it may seem, after all the battles I have fought, I think that was the lowest point in my life. During all those early years when I had fought so hard to overcome so many obstacles, I was young, energetic, and driven by a dream that would not be denied. I had always said that if I wanted something, nobody could outwork me. They might outperform me, but they couldn't outwork me. I believed that was part of the secret of my success. I had done well, but I had paid a price. I'd never coasted into anything. Now I was twenty years older, with a damaged heart, and I was simply tired. For just once in my life, couldn't something be easy? I wasn't sure I had enough "want-to" left to keep fighting.

As always, God came to my rescue. He used a creative pastor and a generous congregation to remind me that he is still in control.

Gwenelda and I had decided we had to go to General Conference in St. Louis this year. I needed the contacts I could make, but we didn't have the money. She said, "We'll go on our credit card. We'll lose it, but we'll get to the conference." I really felt like God was going to provide the money for us to go, but I didn't say anything to her.

The Sunday before the Conference started, we still did not have the money, and I decided I might have been wrong. I was preaching in Pearland, Texas, that weekend for Pastor B. V. Barnett. After I finished my sermon, I went back to my seat and knelt down. I often do that. It not only gives me a chance to pray, but also to recoup, because I had preached hard and felt wiped out. I had tuned everything out, but suddenly I heard Brother Barnett say something that caught my attention. He said, "Folks, if we act quickly, we can be the ones to have the opportunity to send the Oggs to the General Conference." Now, I didn't know what to do—whether to stay kneeling or get up. I decided to stay down. That congregation gave enough money, hundreds of dollars, to send us to Conference, with $15 extra. After that, how could a man feel like he was not in the will of God? Once again, he had shown me that he will supply your needs if you commit yourself to him.

Again, everything is flourishing. My seminars are packed,

and I am in sudden demand on radio talk shows. In one year, I have launched a new ministry, gotten it on a sound financial footing, finished my book, am very busy speaking on the conference-banquet-special events circuit. The Oggs are talking about a new car, moving out of our tiny apartment, and vacationing in Hawaii.

Everywhere I go, I am sharing the message of the "want-to." There is nothing I have accomplished that you can't accomplish also. It doesn't matter who you are, or where you are if you are in the will of God and if your desire is pleasing to God. You will be amazed at what you can gain in him, if you will just simply state, "I want it, I want it, I want it." A prayer life? You can have a prayer life. Witnessing? You can be a fantastic witnesser. You can preach. I don't care if you have problems physically. If God calls you to preach, it doesn't matter what you have to offer him. What matters is what he has to offer you.

When they looked for somebody to try an artificial heart on, they weren't just looking for physical characteristics. They chose a man who was known to have the tenacity and will of a bulldog. When they cut him open and stuck a machine in his chest, he had to have more than muscle. He had to have grit. He had to be a fighter. Barney Clark had learned the secret of success. He knew the question is not whether you *can*, but whether you *want* to. If you want something badly enough, are willing to work for it, and will surrender the ultimate outcome to God, there is no limit to what you can achieve. You will be surprised and amazed at what you can do, if you really have the "want to." If you have the desire, there is nothing that you and the grace of God can't do!

Make a plaque . . . hang it on your wall, hang it on your neck, anywhere you can see it. Read it and repeat it about fifty times a day, "I can do *all* things through Christ who strengthens me." And *never* forget—*You Gotta Have the Want-To!*

Dear Friend,

I hope this book has been, in some way, an inspiration to you. If I can help you in any way, you may write me at the following address:

Allan C. Oggs, Sr.
Pulpit Ministries
3729 West Grandlake Blvd.
Kenner, LA 70065